CW00521779

ECHO
A NEW DIMENSION
By
Michael Dewar
ISBN: 978-1-8384686-2-0

Disclaimer

This memoir is a truthful recollection of actual events in the authors life. Some circumstances have been recreated and /or supplemented. The names of some individuals have been changed to respect privacy.

Published By: -

i 2 i

PUBLISHING

i2i Publishing. Manchester.
www.i2ipublishing.co.uk

PREFACE

As I sit here in my front room writing this book my mind drifts back to my time in the fire service. I had a thirty-year career in Greater Manchester Fire Service and during that time engaged in activities most people can only dream of. This book will shed more light on the things I got up to, the places I served and the people I met, and of course the dogs I worked with. I'm now retired and living a completely different life, but I enjoy it. What you will read in the following chapters is a unique story, but unlike some stories, it's all true.

In the September of 2001, an event that rocked the world to its very foundations happened in New York. The events of 9/11 are well documented, and this book is not intended to go over this subject again, however 9/11 had far reaching implications not just in the USA but all over the world. An attack on large buildings with vast numbers of people trapped and killed, how would the emergency services of that country cope with such a massive drain on their resources and manpower? Would they even be prepared for such an event; well, the answer was NO.

I was born in 1968 into a family already firmly embedded into the Fire Service life. My father John was a Divisional Officer in Greater Manchester Fire Service and had been in the service since 1959 after serving with the Parachute Regiment in the Army. He was a tough individual but considered fair by the firefighters he commanded. My mother Renee was a housewife and occasional cleaner at the local doctor's surgery. I had a brother Gary nine years older than me who had followed my dad into the service retiring as a Station Manager in 2014. We lived in a small suburb of Manchester called Walkden, an area of many green fields and wooded glades, although not anymore unfortunately. Over development has turned it into a concrete jungle, but it was a perfect place in which to grow up and play outside in complete safety. I spent my summers on my dad's yacht that was moored in Conway, North Wales, and at the caravan we owned in the same town. My dad was a big influence on me and after my own service with the Parachute Regiment I decided to go into the family business and join Greater Manchester Fire Service in August of 1990.

The Fire Service in 1990 was still run along military lines with marching and saluting very much on the agenda during training, mistakes on the training ground were met with swift punishments and a sinister atmosphere was always lurking awaiting the next person to screw up. Press ups and running around the yard with heavy rolled up hose whilst having obscenities shouted at you was a common occurrence. Having been in the Parachute Regiment prior to joining the service I didn't find it so bad and only really struggled with the academic side of things. On completion of my 12-week training I was posted to Green watch at Salford Fire Station, a great place for a young fireman to learn his trade, little did I know on that first day what adventures lay ahead for me in the years to come.

In 2001 I was part of the United Kingdom Fire Service Search and Rescue Team, or UKFSSART for short. This team had been set up around 1992 to work alongside the Department for International Development (DFID) for operations abroad as part of the UK government response to natural disasters in and around the globe, such as earthquakes and flooding disasters. It was all done on a volunteer basis with little instruction or training on what to do in the event of a deployment. That said I had already by this time been on operations in India, and had been involved in the rescue of a mother and her seven-year old son from a block of flats that had collapsed in the Indian state of Gujarat. The national UKFSSART team consisted of a number of fire brigades from around the UK whose chief officers were supportive of such a team and were prepared to fund it with kit and training etc. To cut a long story short, this was what the UK had in place in the event of an attack on our home shores. 9/11 changed all that!

Three days after the attacks on the world trade centre, Tony Blair the British Prime Minister gave his famous speech stating that terrorism had reached a 'New Dimension of horror' and all efforts must be made to ensure that if an attack on this scale happened in the UK that our emergency services would be ready, the right equipment, the right training, and the right people. From this speech the 'New Dimension' project was born.

From the minute the words New Dimension left Mr Blair's mouth it was in little doubt what the project would be called. It was to be under direct control of the ODPM (office of the deputy prime minister), and it was to have a huge budget with no expense spared on equipment and training. But who would be trained, and in what?

It was decided that the Fire Service would have the role of Search and Rescue due to its knowledge in this field, the UKFSSART teams would play a vital role and would form the first interim teams until further teams could be trained under the New Dimensions project, and a training infrastructure created in the UK. It was going to take a long time to train people and with no suitable facilities at home it was decided that the first batch of trainees would have to go to the USA to undertake this vital work.

The New Dimension project was to be totally separate from the already established UKFSSART teams. It was activated to respond to terror related incidents in the UK in the aftermath of the 9/11 attacks and would see a huge increase in funding for Search and Rescue work in the UK. But as the volunteers in UKFSSART already had extensive experience in search operations they were the natural choice to form the first New Dimension teams.

Texas was to be the destination for the new USAR (Urban Search and Rescue) personnel, a place called 'Disaster City', about 150 miles west of Houston in a town called College station. With a large university population and an energetic night life it was the perfect place to train, and it was here that I found myself in March of 2004.

I found disaster city a most interesting place and the locals seemed a little strange but very polite. This influx of British fire fighters had taken them somewhat by surprise and they marvelled in our regional dialects and our ability to party to the small hours in bars with names like the Snake Pit and the Prairie Dog. That said the training was hard and it covered all aspects of search and rescue work which culminated in a large-scale exercise that was set over a twenty-four-hour period. It was during this training in the USA that I saw my first search dog in action.

My memory is a little vague now. My recollection of this search dog was one of dedication to his duty, obedience, and an undying willingness to work. I was sold on this idea at once and made a promise to myself that on my return to the UK I was going to train a search dog just like this. Dogs had a lot of advantages over humans when it came to searching; better sense of smell, agile and alert, and not easily distracted when working. No mention of search dogs had at this time been made by the UK government and no plans to have them was in place. This did not deter me one bit and on my return to the UK I started looking for a suitable pup to start training. I was not sure what dog would serve me best, I knew nothing about dogs and had never owned one. Where do I start? I was given lots of advice by people who owned various breeds but knew no one who had ever trained a search dog, so couldn't ask for any advice. In the end I settled on the Labrador retriever. I had been on the net and decided I liked what I had read about this breed, strong, dependable, loyal and above all easy to train. Boy was I in for a shock.

This is my unique story, the gritty, tragic and dramatic story of Echo, one of the original Fire Service New Dimension dogs. Enjoy.

CHAPTER 1

SELECTION

First things first: I must take the time to mention a guy called Rob who really started all this dog stuff off for me. He was on the UKFSSART team in Manchester and had travelled to the India earthquake with me in 2000, and the Pakistan earthquake in 2005, as part of the UK Fire Service search team. He had been to Texas on the initial USAR course and was well up to speed on what was going on in the USAR world. I had met Rob years before when I started my Fire Service career at Salford Fire Station. I liked him at once, as he came from the same military background as me, and we became good friends. He was one of those guys who was always dependable and never seem to flap. He was about 5ft 8ins tall and dark skinned with a laid-back attitude to life, at times he was too laid back. During a rescue in India of a seven year old child and his mother, I commented that the building we were in may come down on us at any time, to which he just said, "If it happens it happens". The other reason Rob was in such demand by me was that he had been training a search dog called Spike, a mad Springer Spaniel that never stopped barking, for about three months. I had done some bodying for him (lying in the grass waiting for Spike to find me), over the previous weeks and months so he was my resident expert in K9 training and selection, although in reality he was as clueless as me as to the right way to go about it.

Rob was a big Springer lover and suggested at once that that's what I should have. I liked Spike, but there seemed to be something about him that didn't quite fit with being a search dog. I was no expert but went with my first instinct that a Labrador was the one for me. My wife, Sue, was also a big Labrador lover so in the end she made up my mind once and for all.

I had no idea about how to select a pup for this work and didn't even know there were tests you could give the pup to see if he/she was suitable. Rob had gone to the local pet shop to buy Spike, but the problems with this approach were becoming obvious. Should I get a bitch or a dog? I had read that dogs were more loyal and that a bitch could be temperamental, but I had no idea which way to turn. It was at this point, just as my head was becoming full of contradictory information, that I was put in touch with a guy called Phil who had been in the search dog game for about 20 years and ran an organisation called CANNIS. This was a charity search and rescue dog organisation which operated in the north of England, with four dogs on the team. It had seen deployments to many disaster hot spots over the years so had lots of operational experience in search dogs. Phil told me, as luck would have it, that he had some Labrador pups for sale that would be prime candidates for search dog training and suggested that I come over and have a look to see what I thought of them. It was at this point, full of excitement at the selection of my first search dog, that I made the first of many blunders… taking my wife along!

I had met her through the Fire Service and the moment I saw her I knew she was the one for me. She had been brought up on the tough streets of Salford, which is a suburb of Manchester, and despite trying to hide her Salford accent she still let it slip when she got angry. She was five years older than me with olive skin and dark hair and was to become my best friend and the backbone of my future dog unit. She was to put up with a lot in the years to come.

We decided to go to Phil's after I finished work on a cold dark January night in 2004, leaving Daniel, our son, with my dad as I didn't want him trying to influence my choice of dog. As we drove north to Phil's, I told Sue that it would be my decision which, if any, of these pups we were going to have. As we arrived, I got out of the car and found myself shaking uncontrollably at the prospect of seeing these dogs. We knocked on the door and I was half tempted to run, but Sue told me to get a grip in her usual way that snapped me back to life. Phil answered the door and invited us in. He asked us if we wanted a brew or anything, but I said I wanted to get on with this before I lost my nerve and bolted. He said that was fine and that he would get the dogs and we should wait in the kitchen for his return. As I waited, I looked around and saw pictures on the wall of dogs Phil had trained. This put me at ease that this man was the right person to be speaking to. As I looked at the picture of one particular dog, I could hear a commotion coming from the rear of the house and getting closer by the second. I visualised 100 puppies running wildly out of control like a herd of Raptors waiting to meet their new master. The door suddenly burst open and in came Phil with five tiny blonde, almost white, Labrador pups. "Here are the boys," he said as the kitchen was instantaneously taken over by these out-of-control hounds, fighting, and chewing almost anything they could. Sue gave out a big "aren't they gorgeous," but I was frozen to the spot. This was real; this was how my life was going to be from now on; no more chill time, no more going out when I wanted. These pups had me scared.

We spent about an hour weighing them up with Phil giving his opinion on which he thought were the best for search work. I was bound by his judgement as I had little idea about what I was looking at. Sue had her eye on one little chap and wouldn't put him down. I kept telling her to get a grip, saying it wasn't how cute they were but if they could do the business. She kept on about how this one chose us and how much Daniel would love him, etc. I had my eye on the meat head of the pack and it was obvious that this guy would be a big lad as he grew up. I had a vision of me walking proudly down the street with this big Lab with some attitude and a 'don't mess with me' sign hung around his neck. I had to keep telling myself that there would be no future unless this dog could work and work well. I tried to speak to Phil on his level and made out I understood what he was talking about when he described how you select a puppy for search work; the right drive, boldness, and ability to be independent from the others, but I was praying he was going to make my mind up for me and make the right decision.

In the end, we settled for the one Sue had originally picked up. He liked to play with the tennis ball Phil had and was a little more independent than the others. He wasn't the big bruiser that I had imagined but he was a good size. He had big, almost black, eyes that compelled you to stare into them and an almost white coat that really was as smooth as velvet. He looked almost too delicate for a search dog. He seemed calm in Sue's arms and I knew that this was the dog for me. We decided to call him Echo because, as always, Sue liked the name, and she got her own way.

As we left Phil's house for the long trip home, he gave us some final advice about our new hound. He told us that if he cried in the night, we shouldn't go to him as it would be our first and biggest mistake. With that in mind we made our way home with our new addition to the family. The trip took about two hours and Echo sat on Sue's knee the whole way. When we got to my father's house Daniel came running out asking if we had the new puppy. It was at that moment that I felt for the first time like a real dad to Daniel, bringing my boy his first pet dog. I never mentioned it, but I felt very proud seeing them on the floor playing with a tennis ball and they were to become the best of pals in the years to come.

During the next few days Echo settled in well, no howling at night which was a relief and very little mess in the house. I had built him a box in the kitchen to give him a den to retreat to when he wanted to be away from us, but as it happened, he wanted to be with us constantly, which we didn't mind. He was a demanding lad and, as Phil had explained when we selected him, he was a high drive working Labrador puppy and would need constant stimulation and attention. I found the routines with Echo a bit demanding at first having never owned a dog before, but I started to grow into the role, I started to enjoy my time with him and found his little ways amusing and dare I say it, cute!

Our routine in the morning started at six o'clock, when I could hear his claws tapping on the kitchen floor. It almost sounded like Morse code for "get out of bed, dad". I would get up and let him into the garden while I had some breakfast. As I opened the patio door he would run out at full speed and have a big wee. He would then just run around in a big circle for about two minutes, as fast has he could, until he seemed to run out of steam: the mad Lab two minutes I called it as I ate my cornflakes and smiled to myself and looked out of the window at him. After he was done, he always came to the patio door and pushed his greasy nose against the glass as if to say, "what's next, dad"? One issue that I had not thought of when I planned Echo's residency at our house was the garden. Our rear lawn was mainly clay-based and drainage in wet weather was an issue, even walking on it would turn the grass to a muddy pulp. One night we had a very heavy downpour. Echo had only been with us about a week when I came to let him out in the morning, he ran out in his usual manner, but this time it was like he was towing a plough behind him. Mud and garden debris were torn up as he ran in these endless circles and I had to slam the patio door shut to prevent the mud from flying into the kitchen. As I stood and watched this little puppy systematically destroy my garden, I wondered how I was going to get him back into the house without him bringing half the garden with him. I eventually decided that I would go outside and try to hose him off in the garden. Not the best idea I've ever had I now admit. As I opened the patio door to allow myself just enough space to squeeze out, Echo's big black eyes locked on to me like a missile locks on to a target. He turned quickly and outsmarted me as I attempted to leave the house. Somehow, he managed to get through the small gap I had left between my legs and entered the kitchen, this was now a disaster unfolding in front of my eyes. Sue was still in bed and oblivious to the commotion. Echo, the now very muddy dog, had not only got into the kitchen, but he had also entered the living room via the door I had left open. The scene was one of total carnage. Echo was running at full speed around the kitchen and front room shaking mud like it was confetti at a wedding. It was up the walls, on the TV and, to make matters worse, was now all over Sue's prized white leather settee. He was having the time of his life and obviously thought it great fun. I, on the other hand, now feared the wrath of Sue as I tried to steer Echo to the back door and back into the garden. As I tried to herd him to the door, I kept reminding myself that getting this dog was my idea! After what seemed like an age of destruction, both me and Echo were jolted back to reality by a loud voice coming from the heavens. Sue had been woken by the commotion and had stood silently at the top of the stairs watching it unfold. After she had seen enough, she shouted at the top of her voice "Stop"! It was like a switch had been turned off in both Echo and me and we froze at the sound of her voice. As Sue made her way slowly and deliberately down the stairs, Echo knew he was in for a good telling off. Immediately, he ran and hid behind me with just his head sticking out behind my legs. "You coward," I whispered to him as my eyes darted round the room looking for my own place to hide. As Sue got to the bottom step, I could see in her eyes that this was not going to end well for either Echo or me. She was calm as she joined me and the now panting muddy Lab on the sofa, and, as she sat down Echo put his paw on her thigh as if to say, "Sorry, mum." This made her smile for a moment, but the hard truth was still pending. She spoke softly and as she did she stroked Echo's head with a calming hand and said, "Mike, this is your mess, clean it up and we will say no more about it, and to prevent this happening again Echo is now banished to the kitchen and banned from the front room. Is that clear?" As Sue left the room, I followed her into the kitchen to do a bit of man grovelling and smooth the waters. When I returned to the front room, Echo had fallen asleep on the now not-so-white leather sofa, I whispered to Sue to come and take a look and as we stood just looking at our new dog, we had big smiles on our faces.

CHAPTER 2

EARLY DAYS

After about two weeks Echo was well into his new routine, so both Rob and I decided it was time to introduce him to his new work. Sue wasn't happy at all and protested that Echo was only three months old and too young to start with the 'search stuff' as she called it. I told her that this was serious stuff and not to get involved, but she insisted that we should let him be a pup and do puppy things before moving on. I decided not to listen to her and got on with the job, but as it turned out she was spot on.

By this point the New Dimensions funding via the UK Government had started to arrive in fire services. The name of the project was an apt one. Although the Fire Service had been using dogs for the detection of accelerants for several years prior to 9/11, using them for search and rescue was a new concept altogether, so the name New Dimension fitted the dog side of the project perfectly. The funding provided equipment and training and also set out a way of dealing with various incidents on a national scale. Due to Manchester Fire Service's position geographically, it was decided that we would share our funding with Lancashire Fire Service. They would receive the lion's share and we would take what was left. It was a strange decision, many of us thought, because Manchester was a major UK city and probably high on any terror hit list, a thought that tragically came true a few years later. Echo was to receive around £2,500 a year to fund his training and upkeep, I was pleased with this but as it turned out that amount didn't even cover his food and vets bill for a year. I also received a new van to transport Echo around, well I say new van, it was new to me but in reality, it was an old, converted fire safety van that had seen much better days, at speed things used to fall off it and at times the gear stick came off whilst using it. I nicknamed it Thunder Bird 1. The New Dimensions project had arrived in Manchester Fire Service and for Echo, our New Dimensions dog, it was time to crack on.

Echo's first experience with other dogs was Spike, Rob's slightly mad Springer, that had been training for search work for about six months. When he first saw Echo on the local field, he sped over to him and nearly took his head off as they collided. Spike towered over Echo and dominated him completely, but as Echo was only just over three months old, I knew the balance of power would shift as the weeks rolled by. Rob and I were total novices at training dogs, and with no one with any knowledge close by, we decided to start Echo as we had started Spike, with some retrieving. This Echo did with great efficiency and speed. It was also very funny seeing his small puppy legs scramble for the ball. We had to use a small ball as the tennis ball Spike used was much too big for Echo's mouth. Someone had given me some advice about training a search dog, which was not to push the dog too hard and make sure every stage of training was rock solid before moving to the next stage. I ignored this completely and went at it like a bull in a china shop. With that bit of advice totally forgotten we decided to try to make Echo bark which was how he would eventually tell me he'd found someone. This is going to be easy, I thought. All dogs bark, it's natural, but I was going to find out the hard way!

The word Rob had used to associate barking with play was "speak". When Spike heard that he went mad and barked constantly. As I approached Echo with his little ball, I told him to "speak", I was hoping for an instant reaction and a burst of uncontrollable energy as he barked for his ball, but nothing happened! Again, I told him to "speak" but he looked at me with his baby black eyes with no reaction whatsoever. Why is this dog not barking? I wondered, it's natural so just do it! Rob saw my frustration and started to take the mickey out of me and my dog by saying I had bought a reject and that I should give it to the Guide Dogs for the Blind to work with. I was getting more and more frustrated and couldn't understand why he wouldn't bark. After about 10 minutes of Rob's constant abuse, I decided to leave with my reject dog and try again tomorrow. When I got home I told Sue that Echo was useless and that he wasn't suited to this type of work, but when she asked why? I told her what had happened, she told me to grow up and just try again tomorrow.

As always, my routine in the morning was to take Daniel to school and then take Echo for his early morning run. Due to Echo's inability to keep away from other dogs, I would take him to the most remote areas to exercise him. This would involve both me and him getting very wet and muddy in the winter months. I always tried to incorporate some form of training on these walks, whether it was a recall or just some direction work. The problem was Echo seemed to be interested in lots of things except what I had to say. Was he deaf? I even took him to the vets to ask if his ears were functioning right and they assured me that all was well with his hearing but suggested an obedience class to tame his wild side. This was a good idea and I immediately phoned Rob who I knew took Spike to a class in our local town and he spoke highly of the results. I booked myself and Echo into a class and waited with anticipation for our first session.

It was a cold, wet, March evening when Echo and I set out for our first obedience class. I loaded him into my car and got all the gear I thought I would need: poo bags, lead and some treats. I was ready and determined to crack Echo's bad habits. As we arrived at the class on a large car park at the rear of the town hall, I was filled with dread. There was an army of all sorts of dogs, 40 at least, large and small. I knew this was going to be a trauma of biblical proportions and braced myself for the inevitable. As I parked my car, the lady in charge came over to me and introduced herself as Carol. She said she had heard about Echo and his problems and would be guiding me through the session. She assured me that she had lots of experience with Labs and, in her words, knew what buttons to press. I gave a nervous smile and thought you ain't seen nothing yet, love! After some introductions, the class got going. I was put in the puppy class due to Echo being only four months old. The moment we lined up along with eight other pups I knew trouble was looming. The class was informed that the first thing we would be trying would be the 'sit'. This Echo did well, and my confidence was raised immediately. As I said "sit" Echo did this right away and without hesitation. Other owners were having problems, but my search puppy was doing the business right off, however this was to be my first and last piece of good fortune this night. The second exercise was lie down. It was easy for any dog and its most natural position, Carol said. When I gave the command, Echo just sat there looking at me. "lie down!" I said again, but nothing. Carol said to give him a command, then a treat. "Lie!" I said and offered him the treat. He ate it with vigour but no lie down. This continued for the whole class and believe me I was the happiest man alive when it came to an end. As I was leaving, Carol said, "See you next week." I said under my breath, "You'll be lucky!"

On my way home, I made up my mind that as Echo was not the most obedient dog in the world, I would not take him again and just concentrate on my search work with Rob assisting. This, as it turned out, was to be yet another epic mistake.

As the weeks went by Echo progressed well with his early training and even developed a good bark. However, as I'd decided to keep him away from any form of obedience class, his control was non-existent. He worked how he wanted to and would not listen to me at all. It was around this time that Spike, Rob's Springer, started to develop some worrying traits during search training. He started to bark at strange and unpredictable times during a search. At first, and with a complete lack of knowledge in this area, Rob and I put this down to over excitement and didn't correct it. Over the weeks, Spike became more and more unpredictable, so we decided that we needed to have some professional input before the whole thing fell apart. At the time the Fire Service nationally were providing no training for the dogs and it fell on individuals to train their own dogs as they thought fit. Not a great situation, but that was the deal.

Round about the time we decided that professional help was needed, we were introduced to a guy called Chris. He had been in the Army as a dog handler and had since joined the Fire Service. He was also one of the major players in the K9 world nationally. He suggested we make contact with a guy called Dave, who was a service dog handler with the police and very experienced at what we were trying to do. At Chris's suggestion, we decided to meet up with Dave as he lived close by. This would let him see the dogs at work and see what stage we were at and what help he could offer. We agreed and a date was set for Echo and Spike to be put through their paces by this competent dog handler. Rob couldn't make the first date, so I decided to go on my own with Echo and see 'what was what'. The venue was a large industrial estate near Heywood, Manchester. It had a large, fenced-in, wooded area that would be perfect for some training. As I pulled into the car park, I was met by this guy who introduced himself as Dave. To be honest he wasn't what I was expecting. He was about 5ft 8ins tall with a sort of calming influence in his voice. I had expected a sergeant major type who would tell me that my dog was useless and to get rid ASAP. We chatted for a while and then decided it was time to get Echo to work. This was the moment I was dreading. Echo had already eyed this guy and I could see in his eyes that he wasn't going to play the game. As I approached the cage, Echo started barking aggressively. I put my fingers on the door release catch, and as I did a shiver went down my spine as I was about to unleash Hell! As soon as Echo heard the catch click, he bolted for freedom nearly crushing me against the door. He was out and free!

Dave suggested that we start with some simple runaways. This was an exercise where a person would run away shouting the dog's name enthusiastically and being generally an idiot for the dog's benefit, then the handler would let the dog go and allow it to chase the "body" and bark at him till the body gave the dog the toy. I knew Echo was good at this type of exercise and agreed immediately with this suggestion. What's the worst that could happen? I thought. When I released Echo to chase Dave, he bolted out at full speed and on catching up with him barked aggressively which was exactly what I wanted. After about 10 good barks Dave gave Echo the ball with a big "good boy" shout. I was so pleased with my dog's efforts and could see Dave was impressed by this mad little Labrador. Unfortunately, and true to form, Echo managed to turn my tears of joy into ones of frustration. He now had the ball and despite my efforts he would not bring it back to me. Dave was eager to continue the training, but Echo was insistent on running in circles just out of my reach and would not give the ball back. I made the fatal mistake of trying to chase the dog, which Echo thought was fantastic fun and spurred him on to keep running around at full speed with me chasing him. After about 10 minutes of watching this mad dog and even madder owner fight it out Dave decided to take direct action and cornered Echo. As we slowly approached this panting half-crazed Lab, we could see its eyes darting left and right as he desperately looked for an escape route. As we got within grabbing range I leapt forward and managed to wrestle the ball from Echo. While I was wrestling with him, I wondered what this professional police-dog handler must be thinking of this Fire Service dog team which at that point were fighting aggressively for a small rubber ball.

As I left this first training session, I wondered where this dog training thing was going. For my efforts I had a dog that would search without hesitation, but without any control. I had a dog that I would need to fight equally as aggressively as any Friday night brawl to get any toys back off him. I was confused and frustrated and didn't know what action to take to rectify this. Should I even continue with this dog or consider getting another? All these things raced through my mind on my journey home, but as my Dad used to say, "have a little faith". In the back of my mind, I knew that Echo was going to make the grade and that I should just give him the time to develop as a dog and as my wife said, "let him be a baby".

I was determined that I was going to see this through and not let it be some passing fad. No matter how hard Echo was to train, I was going to crack this dog and get him qualified in the coming months.

As the weeks went by, Echo's search training started to improve under the watchful eyes of Dave, and we were confident that the dog was on course for an assessment in 2006. That said, I was not happy with Echo's control and obedience, he still did things his way and every time I let him off the lead to search, I cursed the night I drove away from the puppy class thinking it wasn't important. He was such a fantastic search dog and never let me down. However, I knew that unless I got a grip of this out-of-control search machine I would not have a hope in hell's chance of passing any assessment. The obedience test on the assessment was a difficult thing to pass for any dog. As I had no real experience with teaching obedience or control work, I was making all kinds of mistakes with Echo. This was now frustrating me to the limit of my patience, and I was starting to lose hope again.

As I was training one morning in the local park trying, as usual, to make Echo do something he didn't want to do, I noticed a guy watching me from near the car park. He was just leaning against a blue van staring at me intently and to be honest he was making me nervous and I was trying not to make eye contact with him. After about 15 minutes, I decided that I had wrestled with Echo long enough and, combined with the staring stranger, decided to go home. As I was walking to my beloved Citroen van, this guy started to walk towards me. This is it, I thought, I'm going to be mugged by this now larger than life guy bearing down on me fast. I hoped Echo would leap to my defence like some modern-day Lassie and take this guy out with one hard bite to the balls. As he came close, I told Echo to bring him down police dog-style and I would do some kung-fu shit on him. It then occurred to me that Echo would most probably lick the guy to death, and I don't do kung-fu. As my heartbeat got to top speed, this guy spoke. To my surprise, and total relief, his voice was soft and reassuring. He said his name was Tony and he was a professional dog trainer, he also said he had been watching me struggle with the dog and asked if he could help me in any way. I immediately introduced myself and told Tony what I was training Echo to do. He said that he was unaware that the Fire Service had dogs but was willing to help me for free. Now anybody that knew me was aware that "free" was a word that I could associate with! How lucky was I? This guy who trained dogs for a living was now willing to help me tame this wild bear for nothing. I quickly said yes and agreed to meet him a couple of days later. As I drove away, I had a feeling of joy and thought that things had taken a turn for the better.

At his suggestion, we met on a quiet field near his home, because it was unlikely we would be disturbed by other dog walkers and Echo would not be distracted. He explained that what I was doing in my attempt to train Echo to walk to heel was confusing the dog. He said that the concept was very simple and by the end of the session I would have the basic skills to bring Echo up to the required standard. He started by giving me a demo with this huge Doberman that leapt out of the back of his transit van like some modern-day hunting wolf. It came straight to the heel position and looked at Tony, ready for the next command, and started his heel work routine with sharp left and right turns. As the dog worked through its routine, I was thinking to myself that we had a lot of work to do to get Echo to this high standard. I was also quietly pleased that Tony had joined the Echo training team, and knew he was the man for the job of instilling some discipline into this headstrong, but lovable dog.

After Tony had finished his demo, he told me to get Echo out of the van and give it a go. The method was to get Echo to concentrate on a tennis ball in my left hand, and every time he looked directly at me, I was to quickly throw down the ball at him. It was supposed to build up the time between him looking at me to throwing the ball. Echo took to this very well and within 20 minutes of this first session he was getting the idea. I was somewhat impressed by Tony's attitude to the dog and his ability to work Echo just as he wanted. There was no struggle and Tony kept the dog calm, which made an enjoyable and relaxing game for him.

After we had put Echo through his paces, we chatted about what was the best way to progress his obedience training and decided to meet up again in a few days after I had worked with Echo on my own. I was now full of confidence about the future. In 20 minutes, Echo had made more progress than I had achieved in the last few months. He was still as mad as a hatter, but he was starting to show some signs of discipline and control.

In the days to follow, I put Echo through a vigorous training regime undertaking this new obedience technique and he took to it better than I could have hoped. He was walking to heel with the precision of a Crufts champion! It was at this time that I came to appreciate how proud Echo looked during these early days, as he walked with his head up and trotted alongside me waiting for his ball to be delivered. He was transfixed on my eyes and seemed to know just when the ball was going to be delivered. This out-of-control Labrador was now looking more like the search dog that I had seen a few months before in the USA. I was sure now that this newfound skill, along with his excellent search abilities, was going to get Echo to the high standards required from the Fire Service.

With Echo's newfound obedience, I was able to relax and concentrate on his search work a bit more, but one of my main problems was what to do with him while I was working nights at the fire station. Sue left for work early and I didn't want Echo left alone in our house, as we only lived in a small semi with walls so thin I could hear the next door neighbour snore in bed and I didn't fancy any complaints about Echo barking. He was also a bugger for chewing and had virtually destroyed my kitchen by this stage including managing to rip the fridge door off its hinges. It was decided by the powers that be that as he was a Fire Service dog, he was entitled to come to work with me and stay in the station while I worked nights.

At about this time, the Fire Service in Manchester was in the process of removing beds from the fire stations as it was thought that beds and sleeping during night shifts wasn't very modern. As you can guess, the decision wasn't very popular with the workforce who saw this as an attack on working conditions and standards. They were unhappy when they saw what they were replacing them with.

The Blue Calcot chair was a semi-reclining armchair that would have been great for watching TV in for a while, but as for sleeping in it for seven hours it was a nonstarter. It was uncomfortable and gave you back and headache and drove most firefighters to sleep on the floor on makeshift sleeping arrangements like camp beds and blow up lilos. After a 15-hour night shift the station looked like some inner-city doss house with people sleeping wherever they could. I decided that Echo would sleep in his portable cage and stay in the locker room during my 15-hour shift. He needed to be confined due to his tendency to root in the bins for bits of food the firefighters had thrown away, and because West 59 station was one of the busiest in the county, with over 9,000 calls a year the chances of me being turned out were high.

The time arrived to take Echo to work. Sue was panicking and kept telling me to look after him and came up with a hundred scenarios of what might happen to him, ranging from him being stolen from the station to the station catching fire. I reassured her that all would be well and that the lads would love having him there.

Before going to work, I gave him a short run to relieve himself. This resulted in a most traumatic event and one which any dog owner will connect with. The main place I took him to was remote and frequented by kissing couples, to be diplomatic about it. When I arrived, I noticed a car parked up and two people inside, not an unusual occurrence, so I let Echo off his lead and we disappeared into the woods leaving the kissing couple to whatever they were up to. After about 20 minutes, we were approaching my van after having had a nice walk in the sanctuary of the woods. I noticed the couple had left the car park and my van was the only vehicle in sight. Echo was sniffing around the place where the car had been parked. As I didn't want him loose in the area cars moved around in, I called him back to me, a distance of about 100 metres. As he was running towards me, I could see his head shaking violently from side to side as if he was trying to dislodge something from his mouth. I couldn't make out what it was, but it was making a disturbing slapping sound as it hit either side of his jowls. When he drew level with me the full horror of what I secretly suspected dawned on me. Echo had a recently discarded condom stuck between his teeth which was obviously causing him some distress as he was throwing his head from side to side with a real determination to dislodge it, as he did the sound of it hitting his face made me heave.

It was obvious Echo could not move this thing himself and his efforts to do so were making me feel sick. I could also see that it was lodged firmly in the area around his front teeth. I knew my intervention was necessary, and inevitable, and with that in mind I decided to take one for the team, well the dog team at least.

As Echo was distracted by all the thrashing about, I came up behind him and managed to get him in a form of choke hold. It sounds worse than it was, but I didn't want to get side swiped by this out-of-control Johnny. As I got hold of him, he immediately dropped to the floor and on to his side. As a result, I had to follow him down and with one arm round his neck I used my free hand to try to wrestle this thing from his teeth. Unseen by me, and while this was going on, another car pulled into the car park, this time with an elderly lady ready to take her dog for a walk. The first I knew about it was when a small Jack Russell came bolting over to join in the nightmare that was unfolding; the situation was getting worse rapidly. If you can picture the scene, I'm holding Echo in a choke lock while we are both on the floor rolling around like maniacs. This Jack Russell is now trying to get what Echo has in his mouth while biting my hand, and to top it all the old lady starts to get involved out of concern for her own dog. I could feel my dignity ebbing away fast.

After what felt like an age, but was probably only about a minute, the lady got her dog back and stood looking at me in disbelief and wondering what the heck I was doing. I managed to get my thumb under the condom's plastic ring and slowly eased it out of Echo's teeth. By this time, Echo was exhausted which made the task easier. I didn't want to offend the old lady, so I closed my fingers around the offending article causing the contents to seep out on to my hand. This is not my day, I thought. As I got to my feet, condom in hand, the old lady looked at my dog van and asked if I was a Fire Service dog handler. After this, how could I possibly admit to that? I looked at my van, then looked back at her and said, "No, I've never seen that van before" and walked off.

I arrived at the station at about 5.30pm ready for my shift to start at 6pm. I kept the condom incident to myself, as firefighters can be cruel when mickey taking. I was met by a mate of mine, Alan, he was 23 and had been in the service for about two years. He was known as Einstein due to being thought of as less than smart, which was as far from the truth as you could imagine. He was smart and calculating and absorbed all that was going on around him. He was to feature in Echo's early training as he had asked to come out bodying with me. He was also a dog lover and he came over to meet Echo and have a play with him. He reassured me that Echo would be no problem and it would be fun to have him around as a sort of mascot. I hurriedly gave Echo a quick tour of the station. He met the on-duty crew who fussed over him and, in typical Echo fashion, he pissed in nearly every room he went in. Due to the commotion in the locker room that preceded all shift changes I bedded Echo down in my semi-private room, where I slept during stand-down periods and shared with the station officer who assured me that Echo was a welcome guest. Echo's first night went without incident and he even managed to do what the firefighters couldn't and sleep all night on a Calcot chair. It was a quiet night, with only five calls to deal with, so Echo had plenty of attention from the firefighters who were constantly checking on him to see he was ok. After cleaning all the yellow hair that covered the room, I left after my shift ended the next morning pleased that my dog had adjusted well to life as a fire house dog.

As the days turned to weeks and the weeks to months Echo progressed well. We had started training with search dogs from other brigades and travelled up and down the UK on training exercises. The two main venues being a site in Portsmouth and a purpose-built training venue in Lincolnshire that was erected on an old military site. This was great fun for the dogs and well thought out by the designers. It mirrored a disaster zone perfectly. These exercises involved putting people under piles of rubble and sending the dogs off to find them. When they got near them the dogs would bark to tell the handlers where the bodies were located. This was quickly followed by the bodies delivering the dog's toy and then playing with the dog as a form of reward. It was all about the play. It was great fun and Echo loved what we referred to as 'the game'. The one thing I didn't like was the competitive streak in some of the handlers. It was very much a "my dog's better than yours" environment which didn't make for an enjoyable atmosphere for me. It got to the point at one training event that two handlers came to blows. It all started in the pub with the usual "my dog can do what yours can't". I left the pub before everyone else and went back to my tent. I had been in my sleeping bag for about an hour when I heard raised voices and the start of a commotion outside. I jumped up and unzipped my tent to see the start of the punch-up. It didn't last long and with honour restored, the two handlers went their separate ways. Stupid, I thought, but calling someone's dog is like calling someone's driving. One thing Echo didn't like was some of the other search dogs on the national team. He had an intense dislike for Collies and had lots of skirmishes with the other search dogs. He got the reputation as a trouble dog and as a result I had to walk him away from the others, which made me feel a bit of an outcast with the team. He was such a great character, but this aggressive streak was worrying, and I needed to get a grip of it and quickly. One of my friends on the national team was a guy called Steve, who had a rather large Collie called Bryn. In the years to come, Bryn would be awarded the PDSA Order of Merit, a great honour. Bryn was a great dog and a lot like Echo in the way he searched but although Steve and I got on as friends our dogs did not. To be honest, Bryn was a big softy at heart, and it was normally Echo who started the punch ups with him. All the other handlers tried to make light of it but were a bit nervous of letting their dogs out with Echo. After one particularly nasty fight with a dog from Lincoln Fire Service, I decided that it was time for him to be castrated, as I was sure this would calm him down a bit. Without further consideration, and, as normal, without thinking things through, I took him to our local vets and booked him in for the operation. The vets I was registered with were called Pet Medics. It was a chain of vets around the Manchester area. Early in Echo's career the owner, Tony, had agreed to sponsor Echo through his training and cover the cost of the veterinary care, because of Echo's ability to get into accidents and sustain injury through his fighting exploits, It saved me a lot of money. The night before the operation, I watched Echo sat by the fire watching America's next top model with Sue and thought to myself that if only he knew what was awaiting him next morning. Sue had threatened on many occasions to 'cut my balls off' and the very thought sent shivers down my spine, so I decided to let him watch TV in ignorance and enjoy his last complete night.

The next morning was bright but cold as I loaded Echo into my car. I had given him a special breakfast of dry food and some nice gravy. I considered it the meal of a condemned man, but it made me feel better and kept my guilt to a minimum. When we arrived at the vets, I was met by one of the reception staff who I knew well from my previous visits. I told her what we were in for and she looked at me as if to say, "you horrid man cutting your dog's balls off". I agreed but it had to be done! We took our seat in the waiting room and it was as if everyone waiting with their pets was thinking 'you bastard!' After about 10 minutes the vet came out and shouted, "Echo Dewar". I hated it when they did that, it was as if he was human and not this superstar search dog in training. As we entered the consultation room, I was told to pick him up later in the day, because I could not wait or watch the operation. After wishing him good luck I went home. I couldn't settle at all and kept asking myself if I was doing the right thing. After pacing round my front room like an expectant father for what seemed like hours the phone finally rang. As I picked it up, I heard the voice of the receptionist who had looked at me with such contempt earlier. She told me that all had gone well with the op and said I could pick him up whenever I was ready. Even before the words were out of her mouth, I was running out the door thinking I'm coming for you boy!

I waited for Echo to be brought to me. I just wanted to see him and get him home but when he arrived, he looked in a very sorry state indeed and was walking like a geriatric cowboy. I was told he should have no off-lead exercise for at least five days and to keep a close eye on him. I knew this would be difficult, as Echo loved his walks and was not used to being on a lead.

After about three days of watching Echo pace around in my back garden looking like a deranged lion you see in the zoo, I decided that it was time to get him out for some gentle exercise. I assisted him into the van and drove him to a quiet area I knew, where I was sure no other dog walkers would be. After parking up, I again assisted him from the van and put him on his lead so he could not run or move too vigorously and cause further injury to himself. We set off and, after a while, I thought that as Echo was not pulling on his lead as he normally did, he must be happy with this slow plod we were doing. I decided to let him off the lead to allow him more freedom to continue this nice, no hassle post-operative walk, but as I bent down to release his collar, I didn't notice him brace himself in anticipation. It was as if he had conned me into thinking he was still sore and wanted to recuperate with a short slow plod. But, as I released the buckle connecting lead to collar, it was like firing a starting pistol for an

Olympic 100m sprint. Before the lead was fully clear of the dog's head, he was at least 100ft away from me and going like a greyhound in chase of the elusive Lurcher. I cried in vain for him to come back, but Echo was on a mission and travelling at full throttle! After he had disappeared into the woods, I was left fixed to the spot with just a blank expression and a lead in my right hand. How had I been conned by this yellow Labrador into thinking he was still poorly? Did he really have the intelligence to manipulate me into letting him run free? Was he intellectually superior to me in some way? Although I was angry the funny side of the event started to make me smile which soon turned into roaring laughter. Echo must have heard this and thought he was missing out on something. As he came back towards me, he started to put on a slight limp as if to say… I'm still a bit poorly, dad. I gave him a big hug and we made our way back to the van.

The way Echo was now progressing was most encouraging and I was becoming more aware that he needed to be pushed more, be involved in more demanding training searches and more lifelike search scenarios and locations. We had covered hundreds of miles since we had started, and it was obvious that more travelling was necessary before he would be ready. I felt that I had crossed a threshold from Echo being a difficult teenager to this maturing adult, who now understood the nature of what we were asking him to do and he was prepared and willing to do it to the best of his ability. Dave, the police guy, was impressed by the level of Echo's progress and it was decided by the two of us that it was time for him to take the next steps on his journey to becoming a search dog.

CHAPTER 3

THE NEXT STEP

It was now January 2006 and two years had passed since I had the hare-brained idea of attempting to train a dog for search and rescue work. My life had been turned upside down and the former relaxed lifestyle I had was now just a distant memory. Echo had progressed well in the interim period and was now searching with the confidence of a veteran search dog. I know the reader will be asking how I turned this mad Labrador into this semi-obedient search machine, and that's a fair question. The answer is that I don't know. I tried to focus his search drive and coupled that with keeping him in check when working. To some degree this seemed to have worked, but, as you will read later, he still had a mischievous streak in him. Although he was not yet qualified, I was confident that he could pass the required tests if asked. His obedience was still an issue and as it turned out the castration had made no difference to his aggressive tendencies whatsoever. He still had to be exercised in remote locations to avoid fights with other dogs, but to be honest I enjoyed the solitude of our walks and the time we spent together was more precious than ever. Although I never said it, I loved Echo very much and felt safe when he was around.

In the previous two years my 12-year-old-son Daniel had become heavily involved in the training of Echo. Daniel enjoyed being outdoors and around the other search dog handlers and they treated him like one of the team, so for him it was quite an adventure. It was also something that Daniel and I could do together, as father and son, so I was pleased to have him along.

The most important aspect of search and rescue dog training is having a 'body' to assist you. This 'body' is a person who goes to hide for the dog, so the dog can get accustomed to finding live scent. It's a demanding job and one which no-one likes doing because of the need to lie down in the open or be buried under rubble on a demolition site, particularly in winter, when it's icy and cold. When the search dog finds the body it's the job of the body to interact with the dog, after the dog has indicated the presence of the body by barking. This interaction usually takes the form of the body delivering a toy to the dog and playing excitedly with him to ensure it understands that it's done the correct thing. Daniel excelled in this role and became the 'body' of choice for many of the search dog teams during training sessions.

By the end of January 2006, I had decided that it was time to give Echo a go at the grading process to become a qualified search dog. I was just marking time with him and I knew that he was as good as he was going to be and needed to be tested to see if the training we had given him was sufficient. I asked Dave and he told me that it was now or never so I should put in for the test. I contacted the National Fire Service dog coordinator and asked when the next grading process was. He informed me that it would be April of 2006 so that gave me about two months to polish Echo's performance ready for the day he could demonstrate what he could do.

The next two months prior to the grading were hectic, with Echo being bombarded with all sorts of training, ranging from search training and obedience, to fitness training by running alongside me on my mountain bike. The biking was normally a straightforward process over a 12-mile loop, but this particular day this simple process became much more complicated. We were speeding over the moors overlooking Bolton, about seven miles into our ride, and just as we summited a rise, I spotted a lone sheep about 200m on my right-hand side. As Echo was running on my left and looking very tired by this point, his tongue was almost dragging on the floor, I assumed that he would not notice or even bother with it. He was well used to seeing sheep, and normally didn't take much notice of them, but this day turned out to be anything but normal. As we drew level with the sheep, I assumed that Echo had managed to pass it without seeing it, after all 200 metres was a fair way off. I was wrong. At the last moment, the sheep bolted and moved with speed across the moor running almost parallel to me and Echo, who was immediately locked on to it. I could see what was unfolding but was powerless to stop it; Echo made an immediate turn and started after the startled sheep, but in his blind frustration to make ground he ran straight into my bike knocking me off. As I tumbled into what was a violent speeding fall, I could hear Echo yelping in agonising pain. When I finally came to a stop, still in a daze, I could see he had caught his front leg in the spokes of my mountain bike where it was lodged between the spokes and the front suspension arm, and he was lying on his side looking shocked and confused by what had just happened. I turned to see what had become of the lone bolting sheep and could see it still around 200 metres away, staring at this scene of carnage. As I came to my senses, I attempted to free Echo's leg from this entanglement, I tried the old reliable method of just pulling it free, but this didn't work and was causing the dog some discomfort. I then attempted to turn the wheel with his leg still in it, in the hope that it would just work its way loose. Not a great idea and again with no success. I could see Echo was starting to shiver and to be honest so was I, so I had no option but to use my pen knife to cut at least two of the spokes to allow Echo's leg to break free. This was going to be expensive! I cut the two offending spokes and to my relief his leg came free, but as he stood up I could see he was limping and my immediate thought was that I had screwed him up just prior to his assessment. We made our way back to my van at a very slow pace, me moaning about my wheel and Echo nursing his sore leg.

I was advised to ease up on him, as it was likely that I would burn him out before his test phase, so I cut the training days down to three a week, which allowed him to rest in his kennel for the other four days. His leg healed ok after a couple of days rest so that was a big relief, but the new wheel for my mountain bike cost me £400, so that was an equally big shock. It was around this time that a disturbing and sinister event occurred.

I usually trained Echo on my days off work, Wednesday evenings with Bolton Mountain Rescue team and Saturday mornings with another guy I knew from the police dogs, who acted as my second adviser. We used various training locations around the Manchester area, ones that mirrored the type of environment Echo would be required to work in while on operations. It wasn't easy, as finding a place that looked like an earthquake zone was tough. One of the places we had been in the weeks leading up to Echo's grading was a large disused hospital in the Wigan area of Greater Manchester. It was perfect for this type of work with lots of empty corridors and little rooms that provided perfect "hides" for Echo to locate people.

One Saturday morning I was at home and getting ready to go out for a day's training with Echo and my son Daniel. As I was putting the dog in the car my mobile phone rang. I could see it was my police friend. I answered it and he told me that he was over at the hospital site with another police officer who he was training with. He asked me if I could change my plans for the day and come over to him as something had happened that he wanted me to take a look at. I enquired as to what the mystery was, but he just said that if I could get to the venue as soon as I could he would appreciate it. I loaded Daniel and Echo into the van and set off, my mind full of theories about what could be wrong.

As I pulled into the hospital grounds, I was met by my police friend who asked me to come and take a look at something. He asked Daniel to stay in the car as he wanted me to see this on my own. He led me down a long corridor and into the doorway of what was once the child morgue. As I peered into the large room, that was now empty and somewhat eerie, I could sense something odd. I turned to my mate and asked him what I was supposed to be looking at. With a slow turn of his head, he pointed to the floor. I could see it was tiled with a heavy covering of dust over it, but as I focused something truly frightening sent my heart racing. With total disbelief, I could see what looked like the very faint outline of a child's footprints. Now this may seem to the reader like the ravings of an insane man, but I know what I saw.

After staring at the prints for a few minutes, I could see there were a number of them that appeared to be walking towards the morgue. They abruptly finished in the middle of the room, which was eerie to say the least. It looked like they had been made by a single person walking in a straight line. By the size of the prints I guessed that they had been made by a three or four-year-old. I turned to my friend and asked him if this was some form of joke. Was it his idea of fun because I didn't find it funny? He assured me that it was not a joke and backed up his words with the fact that as the dust was so thick, a trace of his own prints would be visible if he had walked over the same ground, but only the child's prints were visible with no disturbance at all either side of them. As we walked back to the vans, he told me that the police dogs had been working that morning in the area but would not go into the room. He asked me to get Echo out and try to send him down the corridor and into the morgue area.

When I got back to the van Daniel asked what all the mystery was about. I didn't tell him as I didn't want him to be worried, but I did ask him to come with me to the top of the corridor to help witness what Echo's reaction would be on entering this, now unsettling, room. As I entered the corridor, I gave my shout out which was now part of Echo's search routine, I called out "fire dogs shout out if you can hear me". I let Echo off the lead and he shot out with his customary enthusiasm. As the corridor was long and not that wide Echo had a straight run for about

40ft. The open doors to the child morgue were about three quarters of the way down. As he ran, my eyes were focused on any reaction that he may show to the room. As he drew parallel to it I expected a reaction similar to that the police dogs had shown, but he ran past the room and eventually came to a door that was shut at the bottom of the corridor so could go no further. It seemed a bit of an anti-climax after all the hype. I called him to return to me and set off to report what had happened to my mate, but this is where it got spookier! As Echo drew parallel to the morgue doors he suddenly, and to be honest disturbingly, came to a sudden halt. He was frozen to the spot just staring at me, almost like a statue. I called him again as did Daniel, who was getting upset by this time, but Echo was not for moving. As we looked at him, I became frozen to the spot and the sweat was now pouring down my face as I pondered what to do next. It wasn't long before Echo started to move, not in my direction but a left-hand turn facing into the morgue room. His tail was wagging violently from side to side and he was emitting a whining sound that sent a shiver down my spine and made Daniel cover his ears with his hands and jump behind me. I told Echo to get into the room, but his vision was transfixed on something else and he wouldn't move. The whining then seemed to stop, and he sat down, tail still wagging, but a lot calmer in himself. Then, as I put one foot forward to move closer to Echo, Daniel pulled me back and said he was scared to go down the corridor, so I told him to stay at the top and he would be able to see me the whole time. As I approached Echo, I could see he was calm but not in the room. He was sat just outside it and staring at a point that I guessed to be the middle of the room, the area where the footprints stopped. As I stood over him, straddling him with both my legs, I spoke calmly for him to get into the room and search it. I even tried to push him in, but nothing was going to budge him. I wondered what he could see that I couldn't, what he possessed that I didn't to see this mysterious object that captured his attention.

I had seen enough and was concerned for Daniel who was constantly shouting me to come back. It's strange, but I felt safe around Echo and when I got near him at the entrance to the morgue, I had an overwhelming feeling of joy and happiness; I can't explain it and have never been able to.

When I got outside, I told my mate what had happened, and that Echo had reacted in a similar way that the police dogs had. We said our goodbyes and the three of us drove home. During the journey, I asked Daniel if he was ok with what had just happened. He said he was, then told me that he had an overwhelming feeling of being happy and content, the same feelings I had when I got to Echo in the corridor. We sat in silence for the rest of the journey, I'm not a spiritual person in any way and I know this story sounds insane. It may be, I don't know, but I do know that Daniel and I witnessed something truly magical that day, something that actually touched our souls.

The grading (test) process for a Fire Service search dog has varied considerably over the years, so I will focus on the original one Echo undertook in April 2006. This process was demanding and, in my opinion, brought out the best of the dogs under test. This test has been watered down a lot since its original format, but that's another story. The original format for the grading process was devised by one of the first USAR dog handlers in the UK Fire Service, who had much experience with search dogs both in the UK and overseas and understood the pressure that an overseas deployment would have on dog teams. He created the grading process to mirror this.

The test was set out over a 36-hour period, with Echo's grading taking place in West Sussex and Hampshire. He was to be joined by three other Fire Service search dogs, Buddy from one of the North West Fire Services, Leo from a Fire Service on the south coast, and Zane who was also based in the south of England. Zane's handler was called Paul, an ex-soldier and a most comical figure who always had me in fits of laughter with his stories and funny antics. He was serious when he had to be but saw the funny side of life as well. I liked him.

Over the next 36 hours the dog teams would be required to carry out six searches, both day and night, over various terrain and locations. The dogs would only be allowed to miss one body out of the many that would be set out for them, so it was a daunting task to say the least. You would have to place your total trust in your dog's ability to search and find a buried person. This would be combined with an obedience test requiring the dog and handler to perform military precision left and right turns with the dog to heel, and a long down stay for the dogs to carry out, to assess how steady they were under pressure. It was going to be the ultimate test of the training we had given them. For Echo, it was to be a walk in the park compared to what was to come later in his career.

On the day the grading was due to start, the outside temperature rocketed to 85C. It was hot and humid, just what I didn't want. Echo hated the heat and suffered terribly as a result, something that would be an issue in later years. On arrival at the first search venue, which was an old disused quarry I could see the three-man assessment team in the distance prepping their notes and getting things ready. The team was made up of Fire Service handlers who had already passed the initial grading process. They were also backed up by an independent assessor from a local police force dog team, who would act as a go-between in case of an issue with the process. All of them were experienced dog handlers who knew what they were looking for in a good dog team. After giving the dogs a final run, I decided to take a nervous pee to try to alleviate the nerves. We drew lots to see which of the four of us would go first. As the venue was relatively small, we had to undertake the searches one dog team at a time and as it turned out Carl and his dog Buddy drew the first search so the rest of us had to go off site so we didn't cheat by listening to how many times Buddy barked. I had drawn the number two slot so was now in a state of panic thinking of the million things that could go wrong. Would Echo search when I told him to? Would he be ok in the intense heat? Would he run off? It was the most nervous thing I had ever done!

After about an hour of waiting, I saw Carl drive out of the gate that was across the yard from where I was parked. He was told not to speak to anyone so he couldn't tip us off as to how many bodies Buddy had found. As he vanished into the distance, I was called forward by one of the assessment team and drove into the main quarry and up to the three assessors. When I got out of my van, I was told to leave Echo in his car kennel and accompany the lead assessor to a briefing area. Here I was given detailed instructions of where the dog search was required and given a brief scenario as to what had happened.

Scenario

A massive earthquake struck this area about 10 hours ago and we have had reports from previous rescue teams that several people are still trapped. The boundaries of the dog search are the far extremes of the quarry compound and the building in the middle is out of bounds. If the dog should enter it you will fail this test. After the dog search is complete, I want a comprehensive debrief as to your findings. You will have 30 minutes to complete this task which will start when the dog's lead is released. Do you have any questions?

Any questions? I had spent the last month prepping for this and now my mind was blank. After composing myself, I asked all the relevant questions: Was the electric isolated? What were the last known locations of the casualties? All the normal stuff firefighters ask at incidents with a few dog specific questions thrown in to make me look more professional.

After the briefing was complete, I went to the start point of the search and worked out which way the wind was blowing by means of my talcum powder bottle, which I always carried. I wanted to start Echo into the wind to give him the best chance of finding the buried victims. I set my stopwatch for 20 minutes, which would allow me a 10-minute safety buffer in case Echo needed to return to an area to re-search. I took a deep breath before placing my fingers on the dog collar ready for Echo to start his journey as a search dog. As I released the collar, I shouted "Away Find" to get Echo on to the large rubble pile that was facing us. My heart was pounding, and my mouth dry in the morning heat. Echo ran up to the base of the pile and just stopped dead. I went into meltdown as it was obvious at that moment that he was not in the mood to go up over the rocky slabs. What the hell was wrong? I thought. Had he succumbed to the intense heat? Was he not up to the task? Just as I was about to shout at him in a loud panicky voice, he made a turn to the left and made his way along the bottom of the pile. As he moved, his nose was in the air and he was looking up at the large boulders to his right-hand side. Pete, who was one of the assessors, told me to stand fast and see what Echo was going to do before acting. Echo had gone no more than 20ft when he again stopped and looked up at the pile. As he did so he started to make his way up the side of the steep incline over the large slabs. He was moving well now with real intent in his posture, but about halfway up he stopped and started to look curiously into a small hole, and as he did, he started barking aggressively into the hole. As if that wasn't enough, he stared furiously digging at the hole in an attempt to see who was buried in it. I raised my right hand which was the signal to the assessors that I was declaring that Echo had found his first casualty of the day. Although I didn't know if Echo was right or wrong, as the casualty was buried deep in the pile, I suspected that he was right and was now filled with a new confidence for the rest of this search. It was at this point that I knew that Echo was smarter than I gave him credit for, because instead of roaming all over the rubble pile using precious energy he just walked round the bottom until he nosed something that was worth expending energy on. Smart dog!

At the end of the 30 minutes, I wasn't confident that I had covered all the areas I had been instructed to do in the brief. Thirty minutes goes very fast when you're against the clock and it was with some trepidation that I gave my findings to the assessment team. I declared that Echo had indicated potential casualty locations three times and that he had covered the vast majority of the areas instructed, including staying out of the building that was a sure fail to enter. The assessors thanked me for my efforts and instructed me to drive away without consulting with the two dog teams still to conduct the search. Unfortunately, they don't tell you if you have passed the particular search and you only get the results at the very end of the 36-hour assessment period, which keeps you on your toes. When I met up with Carl and Buddy in the car park, Carl told me that Buddy had indicated on three casualties and, as he was a really good dog, I was confident that Echo's three indications had been good ones.

After all four teams had conducted the search it was apparent that we had all found just the three casualties, so I was confident Echo had passed the first test. This did my morale no end of good and I could sleep well that night knowing we were keeping up with the rest of the dog teams.

The next day we moved off to a location in Hampshire. This took the form of an old 18th century military fort high on a hill above Portsmouth. It was called Fort Widley and was once part of a defensive chain of forts that were built to defend against France during the Napoleonic Wars and was imposing to say the least. On our arrival, we were again briefed on the nature of the searches we would be carrying out. The scenario this time was a collapsed tunnel complex with many people reported trapped or missing. The dogs would be required to enter the tunnels and seek out the victims. Unfortunately, the weather was still very hot, and Echo was suffering even before the search started, the only saving grace was that the tunnels were cool.

The search format followed as the previous day, with Echo going second. This search was far more demanding than the previous one, with the dogs having to enter a sub-surface environment that was very tight and enclosed. As Echo approached the entrance to the tunnel, it became worryingly apparent that I had not trained him for this type of work. It had never occurred to me that he would be needed for this sort of search, although years later during Echo's deployment to Haiti, enclosed space searches would be the normal day's routine for him. As we got to the entrance, I observed that the opening was through a large archway and down a long flight of stone stairs. I was surprised that Echo seemed very confident and didn't seem too bothered with this type of environment. He was pulling at his lead to get down into this new play area; also, with the search being underground it meant the heat would not be a problem in this dark cool environment

When we reached the bottom of the stairs, I was met by two assessors who asked me if I understood what was required and how I was going to search the tunnel complex. Again, I gave them a brief outline of how Echo and myself were going to search this area, but knew in the back of my mind that it would probably not go quite to plan, as Echo was a free spirit when it came to taking direction. That said, he rarely let me down and had a great nose on him. After our chat I took him to a small opening that was the start of the main search area and, as I looked down the tunnel it was pitch black and very tight. A shiver went down my spine and I could hear my heart pounding. I put a light on Echo's harness to help illuminate the way for him. I had my own doubts about entering such an enclosed space because I had developed a mild form of claustrophobia as a result of the rescue of the seven-year-old in India a few years before. I had kept this quiet because such a condition could affect my continued employment as a firefighter. I set Echo off and he disappeared down the tunnel. I could only see the glow of his light and in the distance hear the ringing of the bell he had on his harness. I made my way slowly down the tunnel crawling on my hands and knees, while encouraging Echo with the words "find him", which seemed to carry a long way in the dark, narrow tunnel complex. I knew I had to hold myself together, but I could feel the walls coming in on me. I closed my eyes to try to pretend I was somewhere else, but the darkness and the smell of moist cool air were overpowering. I could not clear my head of the sounds that I had heard five years before during the tunnel rescue in India: the banging of hammers against concrete; the sound of the rescue team shouting instructions down the tunnel I was in; the deadly feeling of not being able to breath due to choking grit and dust, and the smell, the ever present smell, of death. It sits on your shoulder to remind you that you're not alone down there. I needed a distraction, and quickly. After about two minutes the noise of the bell on Echo's harness suddenly stopped, which snapped me back into the present. I knew that this meant one of two things, either Echo had fallen down a big hole and come to some sort of grief, or he was on to a scent and was about to start barking. Due to the unique bond I had built with Echo over the previous two years, I knew what he was thinking at times before he did. Luckily, it was the latter, and after about 10 seconds of silence Echo fired up into an aggressive bark to tell me he had found someone, the noise of the bark sending a chilling but reassuring noise through the tunnel. I moved up to where he was and rewarded his efforts with a tennis ball. I reported to the assessment team that the dog had found his first casualty and was ready to continue with the clearance search deeper into the tunnel complex. As we continued to move through the tunnel my apprehension seemed to calm down, as Echo was making for a good distraction for me. It sounds funny I know but I somehow felt safe with him down in that dark, concrete coffin, as if he was saying to me "nobody's going to hurt you, dad". Echo located a further three bodies to make a total of four 'finds' for this scenario. I was pleased with Echo's efforts and was proud of him, as he had never been in a tunnel before. I told myself that the training had worked, and this was probably the last time Echo would ever do this type of search. Four years later I was going to be proved wrong.

The next round of searching saw Echo performing well and he was looking confident and responsive. My own faith in him was sky high, and I had a feeling we had cracked this grading process. Although the assessment team did not let on how you and the dog were doing, it seemed that all was going well. After all the searches were completed, the part of the test I had been dreading most was approaching…the obedience test.

The assessment team had decided to conduct this test on a large open flat field next to Fort Widely where most of the search phase had been conducted. This was to be done in two phases, phase one was an individual test which allowed myself and Echo to show off what we had learned about heel work, emergency stops and left and right turns under control, as well as anything else the assessment guys wanted to see. This went well with Echo actually managing to stay with me and not run off, as he was prone to do on occasions. He listened to my commands and responded very well to be fair. I was pleased and knew we had passed this part of the test. Phase two was a very different matter. This was to be a group exercise with the dogs going through similar routines as the individual tests, but in a large group this time. Echo was jumpy at the best of times and was partial to a dust up with other dogs, although not as much as in his younger days.

After the individual obedience tests were completed, the three dogs lined up to undertake the group exercise. We gave ourselves about 10ft between dogs to allow for freedom of movement and to stop the dogs trying to get to each other. As the assessor shouted his first command, all the dogs moved forward in a straight line. It was obvious that the dogs were distracted by the one next to them and, although they were on leads, they were trying desperately to get to each other. The handlers were trying to check the dogs by pulling them in on the leads and attempting to maintain some sort of order in the line. Meanwhile, the assessor carried on barking commands at us: left turn, right turn, about turn. We tried as best we could to maintain the dogs in some sort of formation, but I'm sure it looked like some sort of rabble walking down the road. After about 10 minutes the order to halt was given and the handlers were told to put their dogs in a down stay, remove the lead and walk 20 paces in front of the dog; this was to be the dreaded five minutes down stay. The dog had to remain in the same position for that time, while the handler was to remain in line of sight of the dog and could command it to stay but must not approach it. To say it was the longest five minutes of my life is an understatement. Zane who was on Echo's left started to crawl forward slowly like some sort of beached seal. Echo noticed this immediately and looked at me as if to say, "Can I do that, dad?" I shouted at him to stay and hoped this would have the desired effect. Zane fortunately went static after some encouragement from her handler Paul. With the panic over the reminder of the five minutes passed without further drama. After the time was up, we were told to approach our dogs and reward them for their efforts.

As this was the last test on the 36-hour assessment process, we were told to go and have a play with our dogs and take some time to have a brew while the assessment team looked at the results and came to a pass or fail decision. At least they were not going to keep us waiting overnight as my nerves could not have taken the pressure.

We were called forward individually into a small tent that was set out with a table and three chairs, as I entered the tent I was told to sit down and relax, the assessment team leader said, "Pass or fail Mike, it's not the end of the world." Not the best way to start the process, I thought. The first words out of the lead assessor's mouth were "good effort". In my experience this is normally followed by "but not good enough". He then put me out of my misery and said that we had been a good search team and that we had passed the assessment phase to become part of the operational team. He gave me a sly smile, as he knew the hell I had been through with Echo over the previous two years. To say I was relieved is an understatement, it had meant two years of slog and toil and two years of neglecting my wife and son in search of this dream of becoming a search dog handler. People who have never done it will never know what it takes to train and maintain a search dog. It is total dedication from day one and I take my hat off to those who attempt it.

After the initial euphoria of the result, I phoned Sue and told her the news. She was, of course, very pleased and told me how proud she was of me and Echo and that a new chapter in my life had just begun. She was right. It was to be a new chapter full of tragedy and frustration, but also an unbelievable experience. I slept well that night knowing that I had achieved what I had set out to do.

CHAPTER 4

EXCURSION TO HELL

On the 13th of January 2010 I was sat a home with Sue watching TV. It was a normal night in, me playing on my laptop and Sue watching some sort of crime scene programme. It was cold out and rain was looming on the horizon. I could hear the dogs in the yard at the back of the house and from what I could hear Echo was using Anna (my trainee dog) as a plaything again. I turned to Sue and said that I thought the dogs were getting bored with the lack of operational activity and that I needed to get them out and about more. In the years since Echo's grading in 2006 not much had happened, with Echo being used more as a publicity tool than an actual search dog. He had been on a few low-key jobs; the one that stood out was a search for an elderly lady who had gone missing from her home in a rural area of Greater Manchester. Echo was deployed as part of a 10-man search team and as the rescuers formed a line and moved forward, Echo worked ahead of us at a distance of about 50 metres. About 30 minutes into the search, Echo suddenly bolted to his right-hand side and disappeared down a steep banking. I ran after him and as I arrived at his location, I could see him standing next to the missing old lady. Unfortunately, she was dead, she looked peaceful and Echo and I sat with her until the others arrived. In response to my dissatisfaction with not doing much work, Sue, in her all-knowing voice, said I should be careful what I wished for. Well, in a few short hours she would be proved right! At about 9.30pm, my phone received a text message informing the on-call ISAR team to switch TV channels to Sky News. The UKFSSART team that I had originally joined in 1993 had now changed its name to the International Search and Rescue Team (ISAR). As I turned over the TV, I saw that a massive earthquake had hit the island nation of Haiti in the Caribbean Sea. The quake had been measured at 7.0 on the Richter scale, equivalent to 35 Hiroshima atomic bombs and damage in the capital of Port-au-Prince was extensive with a high casualty count. It was suggested that an international response would be necessary to assist with the search and rescue phase. As I was not on the call out rota that week, I decided to switch off the TV and go to bed.

Haiti sits between two large tectonic plates and is a country that has a history of political turmoil and seismic unrest, after years of dictatorship under such leaders as Papa Doc Duvalier, it had suffered hardship and neglect. As a result, it had a permanent UN peace keeping force in place and was a tinder box of violence waiting to be ignited. It also sits on what is called the Pacific Ring of Fire and is slap bang between two major fault lines, making the region a seismic time bomb. It was into this time bomb that in January 2010 I found myself and Echo heading with just one thought in my head, 'Where the hell is Haiti?'

The previous four years since Echo's grading had been uneventful, he had been used only a handful of times by Manchester Fire Service for search work. Most of his time was spent in schools giving demonstrations for the kids and attending training events around the UK. The New Dimensions Project Echo had been recruited under did not play out as we expected. Millions had been spent by the UK government, but nothing was happening apart from extensive overseas "fact finding" trips for some managers and endless training exercises. All the dog handlers thought that they would be involved in an endless state of operational deployments searching for mass casualties brought about by acts of terror. In the end, thankfully, the search dogs just sat on their backsides most of the time waiting for the call that never came, but on the plus side it was still great to work with Echo and the other dog teams and have the Government pay for it all. The UK Fire Service maintained numerous teams available for deployments abroad in times of international crisis, which consisted of medical staff, search technicians and of course the dog teams. The teams were divided into two groups of about five brigades, each split into rota groups of six months on call and six months off. In January 2010, it was Manchester's turn to take the rota group along with teams from Lincolnshire, Kent, Lancashire, and Wales. The teams were ready for any disaster that came along, but it was the earthquakes that had kept the teams busy over the previous 10 years and as a result I had seen deployments to India in 2000, Pakistan in 2005 and seen some terrible sights that had affected me greatly. When I came home from the previous deployments, I told Sue that I was ok but there was always an undertone to this statement. During the earthquake in India in 2001, I had a bad experience with a young girl who had been crushed in a staircase leading down from a block of flats. I crawled through a tight space that opened into a large void that was the bottom of this stairwell. As I looked around, I could smell this sweet smell that is always thick in the air at any earthquake site. It was known to us all as the smell of death and was a sure sign that a body was not far away. As my head turned to scan the room, my eyes fixed on what I remember as a totally horrific sight. It appeared to be a young girl who was trapped between several concrete staircases that had concertinaed down on to each other. As I stood almost fixed to the spot with fear, I made my first mistake of the deployment. This young girl was obviously dead and only her top half was hanging out of the staircase face down. I should have walked away but I felt myself moving closer to her, my outstretched hand waiting to make contact with her lifeless body. I could see she had beautiful black hair tied in a tight ponytail. She looked about 20 and was wearing a white short-sleeved top and from what I could see a red and white skirt. I couldn't see all her face and should have left it at that, but

I was now totally focused on seeing what this young girl looked like and to satisfy my curiosity I decided to lift her up using the ponytail. Although I could only see half of her, she was so heavy to lift. The smell was almost unbearable as gases started to escape from her body and I could barely stand to be in the same space as her. I was getting lightheaded and my body felt weak and vulnerable in this place of death. As I lifted her level, I got the first view of her face and from the look of her hair and the smart appearance of her clothing I had made a mental picture of what she looked like in life. I imagined a pretty young girl full of life, busying herself with all the things young girls do, chatting, laughing, and looking to her future. But in the blink of an eye all these dreams ended in the most horrific way. The face I saw was a million miles away from the mental image I had made in my mind; it was terribly bloated, and her eyes were almost popping out of her head. It looked like all her insides had been pushed up by the force of hundreds of tons of concrete crashing down on her and forced out of her mouth leaving a bloody mess on the floor beneath her. As I gasped for air my horror turned to anger and for a few minutes I totally lost my grip on reality. I let go of her head letting her slump back into her original position and started to shout at her, telling her how stupid she was and that if she had been a second quicker, she could have jumped into the void I was standing in and survived. For a time, I hated her and kept telling her she had wasted her life. I was angry and upset and ended up slumped on the floor crying in anger and frustration. Eventually, I calmed down and the sound of my voice shouting was replaced by silence as I sat beside her. I started to think about home and how surreal my situation was sat in this destroyed building with a young, dead girl. I thought about Sue and Daniel, who was seven at the time, and what they were up to at home. I asked myself how I could ever tell them about days like this. How could I even find the words to describe it? After a while I decided that it was time to leave this young girl and after saying a few words to her, the content of which I don't wish to share with anyone, I left the building to re-join the rest of the team.

When the call came in to deploy the UK Fire Service team to Haiti in January 2010, it was about 2.30 in the morning, and -5 outside. I was warm in bed in a state of total relaxation. The silence was suddenly shattered by my pathetic phone message alert tone of 'It's a shout, it's a shout'! This noise virtually lifted me out of bed and as I opened the text on my phone fully expecting a shout for Lucy, my fire investigation dog, my eyes widened as the reality of what I was reading sunk in. It said that the on-call team should report to the deployment station asap. As I started to get dressed, Sue told me that it was the Manchester Red team that was on call and as I was on blue team would not be required, but as always, I decided to go to the station to see if I could help the on-call team get ready. As I left the house, I could hear Echo whingeing in his kennel aware that I was leaving the house without him. I shouted to him to be quiet and go back to sleep and I set off.

When I arrived at the deployment station, about six miles outside Manchester city centre, it was full of activity with the Red team busy sorting gear, etc. As I was in my dog van, the team leader, Gary, asked me if I would take a member of the Red team to pick up a vehicle that would be used to take them down to the departure airport at Gatwick. With a disappointed heart because of my exclusion from the trip, I agreed. As I drove a guy called Russ down the motorway to get the vehicle, I received yet another text message, this time it was from the K9 coordinator who was based in Leicestershire. I pulled over and as I looked at the message, I had trouble taking in what it said. It was saying that two dogs would be required for the team and would I be willing to take Echo as part of the deployment. It took me a few minutes to take this in, but after weighing up the pros and cons of the request I decided that this was the right thing to do and with a phone call agreed to deploy my search dog as part of the team. Echo had taken two years to train and with little chance for incidents in the UK and the prospect of a lifetime of school visits and search demos it seemed the only decent thing to do, to get him out there helping the people of Haiti. This is your time Echo, I thought, you're going to make it count.

After dropping Russ off for the 4x4 my attention turned to getting Echo ready for the deployment. I had no equipment ready and even my personal gear was all over the house and would take some time to get together. This, together with the fact that I had to be on the road to Gatwick in less than 30 minutes, made the situation serious. My first job was to contact Sue and ask her to get Echo up and sort out his dog food for a 10-day deployment. This I did with a heavy heart, as Sue worked full time and woke every morning at 5.30 for work. So, this 3.30 am call would not be welcome. As she answered the phone, I told her the news and asked her to get things moving while I made my way home. At first this message didn't register with her as she was still half asleep. She asked me to repeat it, which I did, and this time the penny dropped with a thunderous thud and she leapt out of bed and started getting Echo's stuff together.

As I drove home with my blue flashing lights going at full pelt, I found time to ask myself if Echo was ready for this type of deployment. I knew from my previous deployments that it was going to be tough on me and the dog and that the prospect of finding anybody alive would be slim. I trusted Echo 100% and knew that he would do his best, but would his best be good enough? I guess every handler asked the same question in that situation, so I tried to put these thoughts out of my head and stayed focused by playing International Rescue by Fuzzbox on my car radio.

I got home in about 20 minutes and as usual Sue was in full swing getting things ready. She was always great in these situations and I could not have done it without her. While she got the dog ready, I tried to get my personal gear together. As a former soldier it would be reasonable to suspect that I was a tidy sort of guy with everything in its place. The truth was that my gear was all over the house, a total mess to be honest and, as a result, I was running round the house like a maniac trying to collect stuff as I went: I had lost my dog lead; I could not find Echo's dog boots and all his essential K9 equipment. Sue went about her task as calmly as ever and after getting his food ready she moved to getting my kit together. After about 30 minutes, I told her that I had to go, ready or not. As I stood in the front room of our small semi-detached house, I must have looked a sorry sight. I had a large rucksack over my shoulder with bits of kit hanging out of it, as well as a groggy, half-asleep Labrador which I held on a cut down piece of washing line I hurriedly constructed in the absence of my dog lead. I looked at Sue and she gave me a big hug and told me to be careful and, more importantly, to look after Echo. I kissed her and asked her to say bye to Daniel who was still asleep. I said that Echo would be fine, and he would do his best. I also told her the same thing I told her before every deployment abroad, and that was if anything was to happen to me, she was to take care of Daniel always and love him for both of us. I wanted to say more, but I couldn't get the words out and just told her that the end of my life was not to be the end of hers. This was a sombre way to leave the house, but roaring laughter was to follow within a few seconds. As I went out the front door, Echo spotted our cat, Tigger, sat on the bin outside and immediately bolted in an attempt to corner this startled animal. Unfortunately, he was still tethered to my rucksack via the improvised lead and as he set off like a Scud missile, I went with him unable to dump my rucksack in time. The driveway was thick with ice and as I stepped on it, the power of Echo pulling me sent me pirouetting like an Olympic figure skater but without any of the grace. After doing a 360-degree turn, I set off being towed by the washing line around Echo's neck. He was big and strong, and the thought of some pussy cat pie gave way to his primeval instincts. I eventually collapsed in a heap when the cat outmanoeuvred Echo, but not before I had taken the wing mirror off my car and sustained a large bump on the back of my head due to my ceremonial demise. As I lay in a heap entangled in rucksack, old washing line and snarling Labrador, Sue came out of the house and calmly said, "ride um cowboy." We immediately burst into fits of laughter that totally defused the previous tense situation.

After I got a grip of my senses, I contacted Gary, our team leader, and told him I was at last on the road to Gatwick and would rendezvous with him at the first service station on the M6 so we could travel down in convoy. Because of the distance I had to travel to Gatwick, I decided to pick up a co-driver and for this unglamorous job I chose a guy called Mark, an ex-Grenadier Guardsman who had been on the ISAR team about seven years. He was a big chap with a great character who I hoped would be a good asset on our journey down South. After I picked him up, I switched on my blue lights and proceeded down the motorway to the first rendezvous point, but little did I know what this drive to Gatwick held in store for me.

The snow started to fall and got thicker the further south we went. Our planned meet-up at the M6 services did not happen due to confusion about what services we were stopping at, and after we got past Birmingham we were in the eye of a major snowstorm. Mark had not been much help and had fallen asleep not long after leaving Manchester and emitted an irritating snore most of the way south. The snow got so bad that I had to pull over periodically to clear it away from my blue lights and wing mirrors and give Echo a leg-stretch. After about six hours of arduous driving and non-stop snoring, we arrived at Horley fire station in West Sussex which was acting as mobilisation centre for the Haiti deployment.

The normal procedure when arriving at the mobilisation station was to undertake a series of medicals and complete paperwork to ensure individuals were fit to travel. The dogs also had to have pet passports checked and a vet gave them a through medical to ensure they were fit to travel. After all the medicals were complete and a warm meal was put away, we were given a brief as to the latest situation in the Haiti capital Porto-au-Prince.

As most of our information was arriving via Sky News, we were interested to get a clearer appreciation of what was actually happening on the ground in Haiti. Although I had never heard of Haiti prior to this deployment, I had some idea of the region and what to expect weather-wise. As a young man, I had served in the 2nd battalion of the Parachute Regiment in Belize, in what would turn out to be one of the more colourful periods of my life. Belize was full of delights for the young paratrooper about town. I was based at the main airport in the country, aptly name Airport Camp. This was about six miles from Belize City. Next to the camp was what can best be described as a den of iniquity in the form of Raoul's Rose Garden. Raoul's was a bar that hosted live bands and offered girls for a small payment. When not in the jungle on some form of patrol, I spent a lot of time and money in this establishment sampling the local beer and the local girls; in fact, my time in Belize is a book all of its own. I had a good mate who used to accompany me to the venue and when we were short of cash, we used to pool our financial resources and share a lady for the evening. Now, you may be shocked in reading this, but we were just two very young lads a long way from home.

When we finally boarded the plane at Gatwick bound for the Caribbean, I was nervous about the mission to say the least. I had kept Echo off the plane as long as I could, to allow him to have a last pee and poo. It was damn cold at Gatwick with all the snow, but I had a feeling, things were going to warm up very quickly!

As the 200-seater plane had been chartered for the sole purpose of deploying the UK team to the disaster zone, it only had about 70 people on board, so we had lots of room to move about. Echo came into the main cabin and sat on the seat next to me. I told him to get on the floor during take-off as he was not happy when I tried to strap him in. After take-off, we were told by the captain that the flight time would be approximately 10 hours, so we got ourselves comfortable. I allowed Echo to roam about the plane cabin meeting the other rescuers. He finally settled at the rear of the cabin sprawled out over three seats and being stroked by a rather nice-looking air hostess.

Halfway through the flight, it was noticed that the two search dogs on the flight, Echo and a black Lab called Holly, were becoming distressed and in need of a toilet break, but we still had about six hours of flying time left prior to arriving in Haiti. Because of the dogs training they were not keen on just dumping anywhere, and even if we could persuade them to have a poo, would we really want to sit for another six hours in this airtight compartment with the smell of dog crap as we were eating our in-flight meals? After a discussion with some government officials who were accompanying us, it was decided that the plane would divert to Gander in Canada to allow the dogs off to do what dogs do. The pilot radioed the airport and asked for permission to land and gave the reason why and was duly informed that the landing fee would be $2000 for a plane of this size to land, unscheduled, in Gander. This information was relayed to a senior government minister in the UK for approval and after a tense wait, we were informed that the UK had agreed to pay the required fee.

When we landed, the plane taxied to a remote area of the airfield and the pilot announced that due to visa restrictions only the two dogs and handlers would be allowed off. A ramp arrived and after the doors opened, the dogs ran down it … just in time I thought. What struck me about Gander was how damn cold it was. We had left the UK in a snowstorm, but this was seriously cold. We allowed the dogs a 20-minute walk around the outside of the plane. I felt a bit conscious to be honest, as I could see all the other team members looking out of the windows wishing they too could have a leg stretch. After time was up, we boarded the plane and continued our long journey. After take-off, the pilot tannoyed and said that it had been the most expensive dog shit in history!

The next six hours were uneventful; the initial excitement had faded to a dull longing to arrive and get started. Many on the flight were on their first deployment, but this was to be my third. I knew what was coming and knew that when we landed chaos would reign before any resemblance of order showed itself. At the front of the plane, I could see a group of our managers discussing how things would unfold on arrival. I smiled to myself as I had witnessed this sort of meeting before and was hearing the same bullshit from this meeting as all the others. In the end, I always remember what I had been taught in the Army: no plan survives the first contact!

About an hour out from Haiti the tension rose somewhat on the plane and people started to wake up and gather their thoughts and personal equipment. I raised myself from the three seats I was occupying and cleaned the sleep out of my eyes and as I looked around, I saw Echo still in the arms of his young air hostess. I walked over and told him to follow me back to my seat so I could feed him a little food and get him ready for arrival. As I looked out of the window, I could see brilliant blue sky and clear Caribbean waters below. It looked damn hot even from that altitude and I wondered how Echo would cope on landing. About this time the pilot came on the tannoy and announced that due to issues with the runway in Port-au-Prince we were to land in the Dominican Republic. The Dominican Republic is attached to Haiti with a small border separating the two nations. The republic is rich in comparison to its dilapidated and rundown neighbour.

On arrival in the Dominican Republic, we departed the aircraft and were ushered on to airport buses. My fears about the weather were instantly confirmed, this was damn hot, and I mean **hot**. Poor Echo was cringing under the strain of the heat and bolted for the shade that the bus had to offer. The air was so thick it made it hard to breathe. I knew this was going to be tough on Echo and knew that our adventure had just begun.

After what seemed like a lifetime waiting in the Dominican Republic, sleeping on the terminal floor, we finally received authorisation to enter Haiti. We were told to make our way back to the main airport and load on to a small commercial plane for the onward deployment to the quake zone. I smiled as I got my first look at this so-called plane; it was a twin engined that was very box shaped. It had space for about a dozen people on board, but somehow, we managed to squeeze double that number on it, along with our kit. I had a front row seat as this position offered a slightly more comfortable spot for Echo to lay down, although he was nearly sat on the pilot's knee. It was very cramped and because of the number of sweaty firefighters on board there was no air at all. As we took off, it became apparent that this plane was not suitable for this at all as it struggled to gain altitude with all the weight on board. I wondered who had talked our managers into agreeing this mode of transport.

The flight to the Haitian capital was to take about 45 minutes across very mountainous terrain. Looking out of the window, it was interesting to see how the French had deforested the area during colonial times, leaving a barren, featureless landscape. The flight was bumpy with lots of turbulence, the heat inside the plane made for an uncomfortable ride with many going down with air sickness; after a while, vomit covered the floor and the sight of Echo attempting to eat it left me feeling very sick indeed.

After about an hour of flying in this tin can, we were told that, due to issues at the airport in Haiti, we could not land immediately and had to circle for a while until matters were resolved. This was to be the most hideous period of the deployment so far. Because of the slow circular motion of the plane in its holding pattern, about three miles off the coast, air sickness was becoming rife, with vomit now all over the place, even the dog was looking green around the gills. Again, I cursed our managers for allowing this to go on and I should have realised from my previous deployments that things never go as they should. During the India earthquake nine years before, we had been subjected to a 12-hour bus ride across a vast freezing desert in an old bus with no glass in any of the windows. I nearly froze to death. After another hour of flight, we heard a most disturbing message from the cockpit. The pilot said that due to being low on fuel he was going to go for an unauthorised landing and would run the aircraft off the end of the runway and into rough ground. This news made me feel nervous to say the least and as we started our descent, I felt like I was on a roller coaster ride at the seaside. I feared my end would come in the most devastating of ways, by means of a plane crash. I knew the runway had been damaged in the earthquake and just hoped this plane could take any damage that it sustained on landing. I had used all my nine lives 22 years previously when my parachute failed to open whilst I was serving in the Parachute Regiment, so I didn't have much luck left in the bank.

After what seemed like an age, and a hard landing, the plane came to an abrupt stop at the end of the runway, not quite as dramatic as I had feared, and Echo remained calm during the whole ordeal. As I clambered over all the equipment to reach the door, so I could escape this vomit infested hell hole, I again noticed how hot it was. As I made my way out and on to the grass airstrip all I could think about was throwing up; my mix of emotions coupled with the horrendous conditions inside the plane made me heave and then vomit all over the grass, Echo as usual was right on the ball and the sight of him trying to eat my sick set several other rescuers off with their own version of synchronised vomiting.

The airport was a hive of activity; with planes delivering aid parked all over the runway, with little evidence of procedure or order. The USA had sent in the military to make some sense of it all, but no evidence of this was yet apparent.

When we had composed ourselves, it was time to decide where the UK ISAR Boo (Base of Operations), was to be set up. It was decided that due to the security situation on the ground the safest and most practical place would be the airfield itself right at the end of the main runway. Several other international teams had already set up shop here so safety in numbers was the order of the day.

The UK team set to work immediately erecting supply tents and communication links that would be our ear to the outside world. It was a hive of activity, but one thing was missing. In our haste to board the small plane that brought us from the Dominican Republic into the quake zone, our personnel tents and the shower tents had been left in the Dominican Republic. You may say that this was not a big issue but judging by the size of the tarantulas roaming around in the long grass I felt the security of a tent would be helpful for a good night's sleep. As it turned out, my trepidation about the spiders was short lived and by the end of the day Echo had ushered them all away.

After about an hour of helping to put up tents and generally trying to keep Echo cool, it was announced that a small team from the UK contingent was to go out immediately into what was being called sector 3 of Port-au-Prince. This would be a sort of reconnaissance mission, the team consisting of six rescue personnel and one dog team. Immediately, I put up my hand to try to get on this detail; for two reasons really: one was the thought of getting out on the ground and seeing what Echo could do, and the other was that putting up all this gear and large tents was making me angry in the intense heat, so anything else would be a relief. As we boarded a large truck that was to take us out, I wished my friends goodbye and said I would be back later. As we passed the main security gate of the international airport, it became apparent what the situation on the ground was like. The United Nations peacekeepers were stood in a long line holding back what seemed like thousands of local people from the airport gates. It was obvious that they wanted food or medical attention or were just looking for the next plane out. As we made our way into the centre of town, the devastation was total and together with the burning heat made it a true vision of hell.

As we drove through endless streets in this open-back dumper truck, the sun was beating down hard on me and Echo. Dust was being thrown up into our faces and it was hard to breathe the gravelly ash that it created. I could hear people crying and shouting at each other as if to vent pent-up frustrations. I had a troubled mix of excitement and pity going on in my stomach and to be honest I was nervous being in this uncontrolled, volatile situation.

This was my third international deployment, and I knew what the script would be over the following days and understood that as a veteran rescuer, I could be called on to offer advice and some words of wisdom to the younger members of the team. Soon, a familiar but troublesome smell filled my nose. I had first encountered it many years before during my deployment to India after that large quake in 2000. It was that overwhelming smell of death, an indescribable sickly smell that was all-consuming and difficult to get away from. I had previously carried a small bottle of scented oil to place in my face mask to cover the smell, but in my haste in the UK to get my gear together, had forgotten it.

After about 30 minutes, we arrived at what remained of a small supermarket, a bit like a Tesco express that we would find in the UK. It had collapsed and the frontage was now all over the floor on the street. We exited the truck and after a short brief, and the allocation of two Jordanian UN peacekeepers for security, we headed off towards our first building reconnaissance. The streets were packed with people who had been displaced by the quake or just in shock at the recent events. Easy up to now, I thought, but that's when things started to go wrong.

My experience has taught me over the years that when you get to a disaster zone everyone wants your help, and it's usually the ones who shout loudest who get the help first. As we set off, a young man approached me and asked if I could go to a building with Echo and see if I could find his mother and sister. He had not seen them since the day of the quake, but although he knew they were in a certain building, he could not locate them. I broke the golden rule about splitting the team, but I was glad to get away from the rest of the group as they had been less than friendly to me for some reason. I'm still not sure why they seemed to resent my presence and would have thought that a dog on the team would have been a welcome addition; but in the event, they were not too bothered about me splitting from them. This young man seemed to be in a state of shock and his eyes showed little, if any, emotion at all. I told the team leader that I was going up this side street and to wait for me. I was told to take an armed UN police officer along for safety and was duly introduced to a guy called Alex. He was from Georgia in the USA and looked like he had just fallen out of a *Smoky and the Bandit* movie. He had it all; round brimmed hat, blue short-sleeved shirt and what looked like a *Dirty Harry* magnum side arm swinging from his belt. He also had the accent and no-nonsense attitude to match. We were led by this young boy to the remains of what looked like a library. It had totally collapsed, and I could see at least one body inside the rubble. I asked the lad if he knew where his relatives might be within the building, but I don't think he understood me. He only knew a few words in English. I was nervous as I set Echo up for the search, as this was the first real test of his training under such conditions and it was in the worst conditions imaginable. Anyway, this was it; training over Echo boy, I said, it's time for the main event. I think I was trying to calm myself down as much as Echo. As I released him, I noticed a large crowd had gathered to see the spectacle unfolding in front of them. Echo ran towards the remains of the library and as he got to the front of the building stopped dead on the spot, as he had done during the first search of his assessment. What the hell is up with him I thought, and as I approached him, I could see yet another dead body directly in front of him and blocking his path on to the rubble pile. This was the first dead body Echo had ever seen and I think he was having trouble working out what to make of it. Should I bark? Should I ignore? Poor dog, I thought, but for God's sake make your mind up quick. As it happened, Echo remembered his training well and decided that although this looked like a human it certainly didn't smell like one after three days exposed to the heat and moved on. He traversed the rubble well, but the training we had done had not mirrored this type of devastation in any way. Echo managed to do his best but was struggling with the heat and energy-sapping nature of this collapsed building.

During the search Echo, unfortunately, did not locate the lad's family and I felt sorry for him as I told him the news. I felt even worse when he thanked me for trying and offered me a bar of chocolate. I told him thanks, but he needed it more than me. After the search, it was obvious Echo had used up a lot of energy. This does not look good, I thought to myself, just one search completed, and he's knackered. We had a good few hours ahead of us yet, so something had to be done. It was decided that walking from job to job was a non-starter because of the intense heat. Alex came up with the solution in the form of an air-conditioned UN police vehicle, a huge 4x4 that was driven by a very pretty Chinese UN police officer who had problems saying the word Echo and pronounced it Veco. The rest of my team had long since departed the scene, leaving me with the two officers. It was agreed that we would just travel round the capital searching buildings as and when we were flagged down. As it turned out, this was by far the best way to utilise Echo's skills.

As we moved through the devastated streets it was sobering to see an entire population on the move, but moving where was the question, I asked myself. Where were these people moving to? No aid camps had been set up and no additional accommodation sorted out; it was just a mass exodus of people, stampeding without order and mission. A human tragedy on a grand scale was unfolding in front of my eyes and I wondered how such a small contribution by Echo and me could stem this human tidal wave of misery.

As we drove along the sea front, I could see from my position in the back seat a large industrial complex in front of me, a sort of large warehouse was visible, but it was obvious that the rear end had collapsed during the shaking from the earthquake. As we passed by a young man ran out nearly being knocked over by our vehicle, the hard braking causing Echo to end up lodged between the two front seats, which our Chinese driver found most amusing. Alex wound his window down from his front seat position and enquired as to the problem. It appeared that the manager of the warehouse had not been seen since before the earthquake and this young guy was concerned for his welfare. It was difficult to understand the guy due to his very broken English, but it was clear he had tried to search the building himself judging by the number of cuts to his body. I almost found the situation bizarre, a local, speaking broken

English to a Chinese driver and an American police officer whose own accent was difficult to understand at the best of times. It looked like it was down to me to sort out the translation issues.

After some confusion, I latched on to what this guy wanted. He kept tapping Echo on the head as if to explain what his intentions were. I told Alex that we could spare a bit of time to carry out a dog search of the collapsed part of the building. I asked the young guy what his manager was called, so I could shout out his name as I went through the building, a vain hope I know but it somehow made me feel better to suggest it.

After I had prepared Echo, with a small drink and his PPE on him in the form of his boots, I moved to the part of the warehouse that would be the easiest route for Echo to enter the building. I didn't want him exerting any more energy than was necessary; it was too hot for that. Due to the amount of twisted metal and other snag hazards, I had decided to leave Echo's search harness off him in case it got caught up. It turned out to be a good call. I was informed that the missing manager would, if still in the building, be the only person inside.

I set Echo off to work in the tried and tested way of shouting out that a Fire Service search dog was entering the building. This not only alerted people around, but also worked the dog into a frenzy which was exactly where I wanted him. Echo shot off his lead and instead of making his way through the main front door and, to be honest the path of least resistance, he managed to clamber on to a corrugated roof that was now at a 45-degree angle with its bottom half touching the floor. This led him into what remained of the first floor. As he entered the building, I could hear the sound of breaking glass as Echo made his way forward. He disappeared into the maze of tangled metal and upturned office furniture. I knew leaving his harness off had been a good move. I didn't need any dramas with injured dogs on the first day.

As I stood outside the building, I could hear Echo's bell which was tied around his neck, a neat bit of kit that gave me an idea of his location when he was out of my sight. The last thing I wanted to do was enter an unstable building trying to find my missing dog. This bell allowed me to track his movements by the sound. I could hear the bell faintly, which told me that Echo was deep into the building and still searching well, despite the heat and horrific conditions inside. Occasionally, he would pop his head out of broken windows just to see if I was still waiting for him. As he did so I shouted to him to get back in, as I feared that he would be cut to shreds by the pieces of broken glass I could see. After about 30 minutes, I could hear by the bell sound that Echo was now slowing down and I turned to Alex, who was still sat in the air-conditioned jeep, and said I thought that was enough. If Echo had not found anyone by now, the manager was either dead or had joined the tide of human misery wandering around the city. Alex agreed and I called Echo back. Amazingly, he had only sustained a small cut to his nose which was easily treated at the scene.

As I was putting Echo back into the rear seat of our jeep, I could see the young lad who had originally flagged us down. I knew that I was going to have to tell him the bad news and the sooner the better. I walked over to him and said that we had done our best and that the dog had not found anyone alive. I tried to soften the blow by saying that the manager may have got out prior to the earthquake, but I'm not sure my words of comfort had the desired effect. I was still stunned by the devastation around me and my words didn't seem to fill the void of misery.

The pace and operational tempo of the first day had been brutal. No training was going to prepare you for this; the heat and the smell were overpowering, and I was physically drained and numb by this stage and longed for a shower and some rest.

Late in the afternoon, I caught up with a bus load of UK rescuers. In my absence from the Boo (Base of Operations), the rest of the team had been deployed and were being ferried around in what looked like an airport transfer bus. I managed to smile to myself and thought about me and Echo travelling around in this rough and ready 4x4 with two eccentric UN police officers. I looked at Echo, smiled and said, "We are hard-core, mate."

The last job of this eventful first day, was a dog search of the British Embassy building near the centre of town. It was reported that a British national was possibly trapped and a big effort was underway to locate her. Again, it was totally devastated and didn't look much like a building anymore. By this time, Echo was totally knackered after undertaking about 12 searches during the day and had little energy or enthusiasm for one last effort. I searched part of the building which sapped Echo's last bit of energy, but after failing to locate anyone I handed the dog search over to a dog team from the USA and put Echo away to rest.

The next few days in Haiti followed the same pattern. At first our sleep tents didn't turn up and we had to spend the first couple of nights lying on the ground with a plastic sheet over us for protection, then when they did arrive it was noticed that the shower tents had been left in the UK by mistake, so we couldn't shower or wash ourselves effectively. I understood that these issues were trivial compared to what the locals were going through, but still annoying. The plan for each day was delivered at morning briefings and it turned out that Echo was required to go out every day with one team or another to undertake searches of collapsed buildings. To be honest, so many buildings had collapsed we could have just walked out of the gates of the airport and been able to start immediately, but it was necessary to be transported to the more urgent areas and this was mostly done by the now infamous airport bus I had encountered on the first day; a rickety old shit heap that looked like it had seen better days. We were escorted by a Special Forces contingent from the UN. Every morning we would load far too many people on this bus, as well as some equipment and, of course, the two search dogs, we then had to make our way into the capital under armed guard. It was on one of these epic journeys that the funniest and, at the same time most dangerous encounter happened for me and Echo.

The early hours in Haiti are cool, but the looming sun brought a stark reminder of what was soon to arrive in the form of a ruthless fireball that was difficult to escape and, by mid-day, could burn the hide off a buffalo. By mid-afternoon on the fourth day of our deployment, things had started to settle down for the rescue teams and a routine had been established. The situation was every bit as bad as the first day for the population, but for me and Echo our task had now become more focused with less of the confusion we encountered in the early days. On this day around lunchtime, we had returned to the transport bus for a short rest and some food after a few searches. On the bus were a collection of rescuers and two Canadian dog handlers, the names are forgotten to me now, but they were two ladies, one around 50 and the other in her mid-20s. They represented some charity search dog team back home in Canada and were situated in the next tent to me back in the Boo area. The older woman was very chatty and, as with most dog handlers, thought she knew all about dog training. The younger one was quiet and looked apprehensive and a bit overwhelmed at what was going on around her. As usual, I tried to chat up the younger one, but she dismissed my advances totally so I concluded she must be a lesbian. As Echo had been doing most of the dog work in our designated sector of the city, they had not had much opportunity to get on the ground with their dogs and have a go, so I told them that after I had rested Echo a while I would take them out and let them have a go at a building search. The older woman seemed eager, but the younger girl was not impressed at the thought of stepping out of the relative safety of the bus and into this mass of moving bodies, which was unpredictable at best. After about 30 minutes, I said that I was rested and that it was time to see what the Canadian dogs could do. The three of us got up and started to make our way off the bus, but as we did the sound of gunfire came from over my right shoulder and seemed so damn close. I could almost taste the gunpowder. Three shots rang out in quick succession followed by another two. I knew that the shots had been from different weapons, so was aware of a potential gun battle unfolding near our location. Instinctively, I hit the floor of the bus and in a moment of madness pulled Echo on top of me for protection; my Army training came back instantly, keep low and crawl. Thoughts of being cornered on this bus seemed grim, others had hit the deck as well, but some less enlightened people were just stood up looking out of the windows like gormless morons. One guy shouted at them to get down, the two Canadian girls had followed my lead and had taken cover, the older one was composed, but the younger one was screaming, and she was starting to piss me off. I told her to shut up as her screaming may draw fire from whoever was taking aim at us. I wanted to tell her that dying here was not in my plan. I had always dreamed of dying in my late nineties whilst snorting cocaine off a prostitute's breast. As the gun battle continued, it was noted that our so-called Special Forces security escort from the Middle East UN contingent had done a runner leaving us to our fate. As I was trying to make myself as flat as possible, with the chaos of the screaming girl and the barking dog around me, I asked myself if I was still cut out for this. I had a mixed feeling of fear and anxiety, which I didn't seem to have had in my youth. As young people we think we are invincible, and after several close scrapes whilst in the Army I was sure I was not on God's list just yet. But now, faced with this escalating situation, I wasn't so sure anymore.

After what seemed like ages lying somewhat nervously on the floor of the bus, all went quiet, even the hysterical Canadian had had enough and looked like she had gone to sleep. A local Haitian police car pulled up outside the bus and three officers got out. I say officers, they had a mild resemblance of police officers but looked more like an out-of-control drug gang to me. They entered the remains of a local bank and proceeded to pull two individuals out from inside. They made them lie on the ground with hands behind their heads and beat them with large clubs. It was a sickening sight and as much as I wanted to stop the carnage, I knew better than to get involved with these trigger-happy individuals. After a short but very brutal beating a large open backed 4x4 turned up with what I can best describe as local thugs inside it. The two men were bundled into the back and driven away, still being beaten as they went. I feared that the future was going to be short and painful for them.

The gunfight at the bank had left both me and Echo shaken. I was a firefighter for God's sake not a soldier. I was angry, yet again, at having been put in that position by my leaders, definitely a Health and Safety issue I chuckled to myself. Being a member of ISAR mostly involved attending a series of courses around the world, being used as target practice was a course I had not heard of before but felt fully qualified after this incident.

That night in camp, the Canadians announced that they were going home on the next transport out of Haiti. Too risky was the reason they gave. I didn't blame them to be honest and wished them well on their journey. They left me all the dog food they had and a large tent that I soon moved into as more space was required for Echo to move about. After their departure, my corner of the camp was empty with only a UK NGO (Non-Government Organisation) group to keep me company. This group numbered about 10 in total, all volunteers, but they were a well-meaning charity rescue group who had travelled to Haiti at their own expense from the UK. They worked totally independent of the Fire Service team. I had met the two leaders before when they were setting up the group and were thinking of having dogs in the mix with them. They had a very good looking young girl with them who used to sit with me and Echo in the evenings and talk about a multitude of subjects over a brew. The problem for this group was that they were not liked by some of the other teams for some reason; politics reaches into disaster zones as well as any other area. The Fire Service rescue team had been reluctant to give them any supplies when things started to run out for them in the closing stages of the deployment. I didn't bother either way with the politics and secretly supplied my good looking brew mate with all she needed out of my own vast stock of acquired items, such as crates of Coke and other desirable items I had scrounged off other teams. I was the classic scrounger and on arrival made contacts with other international teams, for some of life's luxuries. One thing that life has taught me, if you don't ask, you don't get. I acquired scented soap from the Mexicans, very tasty food rations from an American team, pizza bases from the Italians which I swapped with a Cuban team for some very large cigars, which I, in turn, traded on for a pair of expensive boots from a team attached to the Israeli Army. My day always started with a walk round this now very large camp with Echo, just making contacts and seeing what was on offer. Echo was a great ambassador in this scenario as all the other teams seemed to love him and it was funny to hear all the different languages trying to say his name. If some of our team wanted to play Boy Scout and go native, good luck to them. I didn't and ended up with a large stock of needy items. As it turned out, this NGO group and its team members were to have a profound and lasting impression on me and Echo, and one for which I will be forever grateful.

On day eight of the deployment, I was out with Echo searching a large building on the outskirts of town, on the side of a mountain. It was around mid-day and very hot and as Echo was moving over the rubble, I noticed him stumble. He looked like a Saturday night piss head who was looking for the last taxi home. He was obviously in some distress, as he got to the top of a large collapsed building, and in full exposure to the belting sun, he just spun round in quick time and keeled over on to his side. I immediately knew this was serious and got to him as quickly as I could. His eyes had disappeared and only the white bit could be seen. He was panting violently and was in a total daze. I managed to lift his lifeless body assisted by Alex, my UN police driver, and get him into some sort of shade. I knew that cold water would not be enough to bring him round again. I knew that time was of the essence and if I didn't do something soon, he was going to die of heat exhaustion; something for which Sue would never forgive me. We bundled him into the police vehicle we were travelling in and I told the driver to get back to the airport asap. We drove as fast as the crowded roads permitted. I could see life ebbing out of Echo, as he had now virtually stopped breathing and was totally unresponsive. I told Alex to pull over as I was going to start CPR and would need his help. He screamed at me that the airport was only two minutes away and just to hold on, but I was more determined than ever in my life to keep my promise to Sue and Daniel and bring Echo home safe. As we got to the gates of the airport, we were stopped by security guards from the US Army who had taken over the place. I told them that we had a search dog in distress and to let us through without delay, but as luck would have it, we had got the only jobsworth in the US Army standing in our way. He insisted on seeing Echo himself and was taking his time about it. At this point my blood boiled over and I quietly informed him that if he didn't let us through and this dog died, I would personally insert his weapon, barrel, bolt, and all up his backside and make sure that the Commanding General of the 82nd Airborne Division of the US Army would be personally informed of the circumstances surrounding the death and that his ass would not touch the ground. He soon realised I was very serious and let us through. As we raced through the camp, I shouted at people to get out of the way. We pulled up outside the UK Boo and unloaded Echo into the arms of some of our team who had been informed of Echo's condition. He was now almost dead, and I could see him slumped over the arms of one of my team members. I knew this situation was getting out of hand and fast as we got him under shade the camp doctor assisted me in getting some oxygen into him by means of the medical equipment we had at our disposal. Soon, we had several people working on him, but as they were all doctors and nurses with no veterinary experience, they were only doing what they thought was the right thing. Much discussion and raised voices were adding to the tension as I took Echo's head it my hands and could see him slowly dying in front of me. One of the rescue team suggested I waited outside, but I was staying. If he was to die, I wanted his last memory and smell to be of me. I could see his breathing starting to fade and I heard a doctor calling for a defibrillator, the demanding manor in which he asked for it gave me an indication of what was unfolding here. I was starting to panic, and the seriousness of the situation hit me hard. We needed a vet, but as the UK team at that time did not deploy a vet with them, all we had was the camp medical team who were already doing their best. At this point, Echo's luck changed when a team member from the NGO charity team I mentioned earlier came over to see what all the commotion was. When he understood the situation, he informed us that one of his team was a vet and, as luck would have it, was sat in his tent reading. I shouted at him to go and get him. He ran over to his tent and brought him over and immediately he took over the situation. He was fantastic, he knew just what to do and barked orders at the other medics who I could see were as relieved as me to have him there. I was elated that Echo was now getting the proper care he deserved. The vet immediately put the defibrillator to one side saying, "we don't need that" and started to put Echo on a drip for fluid loss. He also gave him some drips in his mouth to help bring him round. To say this guy was great was an understatement, as he was professional and had a calming, reassuring tone to his voice. He said that Echo was suffering from an extreme case of heat exhaustion and the next 12 hours would be critical. He needed to be kept on the drip that was now feeding him fluid via his front leg and, above all, he needed rest. He gave Echo a full examination looking into his eyes, listening to his shallow breathing, and gauging his level of dehydration. He also asked about my feelings and said that I had kept my head well during this traumatic event. He didn't know that I was a shaking mess inside.

After all the commotion was over, I carried Echo over to my tent. The guys from Lancashire Fire Service who were part of the UK team had taken the time to erect a sunshade for Echo to sit under during his rest period, a very well-constructed shade it must be said. He had a nice comfy bed and a cool battery-operated fan on him to allow him to lounge in cool comfort. The vet, whose tent was only about 20ft from mine, came over every hour to check on him and declared that Echo was recovering well from his ordeal, but should not be worked until he was fully fit. I explained that Echo was one of only two search dogs in the UK team and I had to balance his welfare against the need for him to search for buried victims. People were depending on him and I needed some degree of latitude about when he could work again. I knew Echo was a tough mutt, only a Manchester dog can be dumb enough to get heat exhaustion, yet tough enough to survive it.

After a few days, it was decided that Echo was at least 75% fit, he was still a bit slow but was chasing his ball and I thought much better than he had been. After some consultation with the vet, it was agreed that he could do some light work again but must not be overworked. The routine of going out and finding nobody alive was becoming tedious. Echo was recovering from his bout of heat exhaustion but was still not 100% fit. I worked him but watched he didn't overdo things. The heat was not the only thing causing him problems, the water had given him mild shits which didn't help, and he had several facial cuts caused by twisted metal sticking out of buildings that had collapsed. He looked a sorry state, but to be fair most of the rescue team were feeling the strain by this time. Due to the lack of live finds in the rubble, I started asking rescue workers to go and hide to give Echo something to find and it was amusing to see how happy he was to play with someone when he found them. Most of the buildings Echo searched had many dead people inside them. One school I searched had more than 70 children and teachers all dead inside, which was not a pleasant environment to be in and gave me huge problems in the years to come. The children looked so innocent and helpless and had died in the most horrific way, one young boy was still clutching his lunch box, the sight of this was too much for me to handle. But that's another story.

One of the most amazing and, it must be said, luckiest rescues we did, was of a young man from a Turkish rescue team who had become trapped by the hand. We located him by pure luck in a remote village on the outskirts of the capital. He had been using a car jack to lift a large slab of concrete, which I estimated to weigh well over a ton; as the jack got to its maximum lift it collapsed, dropping the full force of the slab on this guy's right hand crushing it flat. I was with two guys from a French team who we were using as interpreters, although even they struggled with the Creole dialect the locals used. Because it was starting to go dark, we had to make some quick decisions, as being out after dark was not an option as it was not safe. The sound of gunfire was already starting to be heard in the distance; leaving the guy trapped by the hand was not an option. We also had no tools apart from a slightly dazed search dog. One of the guys suggested we try to free him by attempting to cut off his hand at the wrist. His hand was crushed totally flat anyway, so how hard could it be? At first, I laughed at this suggestion until it dawned on me that he was serious. He said he had a Leatherman tool pen knife that was very sharp. I said if we did this amputation he could die, and I was not even sure a pen knife could do the job anyway. Surely you would need some form of bone cutting tools. After some heated discussion, it was agreed to carry out the planned amputation. I explained to the young Turkish guy what was happening and that it was our only option. He could speak some English, so told us to get on with it and he would just take the pain. Brave kid, I thought, but I was not happy at all about this situation. I informed the group that I would not do the cutting but was willing to knock the guy out with a punch to the head to save any pain that was coming his way. As we prepared our Hammer House of Horrors-style amputation, I noticed it had gone completely dark and as no street lighting was available, we would be working from head torches which added to this unfolding drama. In the dark, away from the others, I took a few practice swings to ensure I knocked him out with the first punch. When I returned, I could see the other two guys looking closely at the pen knife and running their thumbs down it and smiling like some medieval executioners, but, in reality, they were as nervous as me. I felt sick and wanted the ground to swallow me up. As we were setting ourselves up, Lady Luck shined on us. In the distance I could hear a vehicle, or maybe two? I told everyone to be quiet and not to make ourselves obvious until we knew who it was. As the sound got closer, I could see the outline of what looked in the dark like two 4x4 vehicles. As I crouched behind some fallen debris, I could see the two vehicles getting closer and could now make out a large UN logo on the leading vehicle. This was my opportunity, not only to get out of here, but also to save the young Turkish guy from his fate at the hands of the two French "surgeons". I tied Echo to a small tree, and as the vehicle got almost parallel to me, I jumped out of my hiding place nearly being run over by the lead truck. I shouted for it to stop and in a squeal of brakes and a sea of dust the convoy came to a halt. I walked over to the lead truck and informed them of the situation and that we needed urgent help. The vehicles had a small contingent from a South American search team, who were only too willing to get involved and had the tools to extract this trapped guy without the horrors of the original plan. As I sat watching them work, they offered me some spicy South American rations that they were carrying. I accepted as I was starving but came to regret it the next morning.

A few days later, I was summoned to our command tent and was told that an Israeli doctor wanted to speak to me. As I entered the room, he introduced himself and explained that he was part of a field hospital that had been set up on the airfield to treat injured locals. He told me that he had treated the young Turkish guy the night he was brought in. He told me that he was doing fine but had lost his hand as it was beyond repair. I kept our DIY amputation story to myself. He then said something to me that suddenly made my time in Haiti all worth it. He told me that he had heard all about the amputation idea from the young guy himself, and I had been the one to oppose it and delay it long enough for the rescue team to find us. I was a bit less happy at how the guy described me to the doctor: the guy with the scabby looking dog was his description. Having said that, Echo was looking more like the wild coyote every day. He said the young Turkish guy would be forever grateful for this and to pass on his thanks. He also told me that had we carried out the plan, the young guy would almost certainly have bled to death. The rescue team in the 4x4s, combined with my arguing with the two French guys had saved the day. I shook his hand and we parted. As I left the tent, I was pleased that my actions were sending at least one person back to their family alive.

I passed my time in camp as usual during rest periods, travelling from team to team scrounging luxury items: more crates of Coke, shower gels and exotic rations from the Columbian team, as well as some military items from a US Special Forces unit that had set up shop some distance from our Boo area. My donated tent was now full of all things necessary for a comfortable deployment. I even managed to secure a canvas bath which I swapped for five Fire Service t-shirts with logos on them. It was a great deal, and it goes without saying Echo loved his new bathing arrangement.

Halfway through the deployment, the UK team was asked to look at a village about 60 miles from Port-au-Prince, to see if any work could be done to secure infrastructure and search for survivors. Now, instead of sending a recce party to the village consisting of a few people to see what work needed to be done, they decided to up sticks the whole UK team and load all the stuff on to trucks; a decision that made mine and many other people's blood boil. Echo was working again, but not at full steam and a long journey was the last thing he needed. It had only been a few days since the incident on the rubble pile and I was keen to keep him out of harm's way as much as I could. In short, the whole team moved the 60 miles to the new location, spent about three hours wondering aimlessly round the village, then, on deciding nothing could be done, moved the 60 miles back. A great example of not thinking things through before making a decision.

About two days before the end of deployment, the camp got notification of a large supermarket complex called the Caribbean market, just outside the centre of the capital city that had collapsed during the earthquake. Reports from locals indicated that noise had been heard from within the collapsed building. Such reports from locals are unreliable at best, but still must be checked out. Several other international teams had already searched this building over the previous days including teams from the USA and Iceland. Echo was not yet fully fit, but he was definitely back in the game. He looked war-torn now after his ordeal and was thinner with visible damage to his face and body due to injuries sustained whilst searching. He looked tough to be honest and my thoughts turned to what a great search dog he had grown into. He was alert and his nose was constantly in the air, which I knew was a good sign. I could see that he was eager to get the job done and start 'the game', as we called it.

As I sat on the bus heading to this new job, I turned round to look at the team. I was sat at the front with Echo and could see most of them; it was a sight to behold. They looked drawn and tired; you could almost see the tragedy on the individual faces. I wished I could have taken a picture; if I could describe it, it would be an overcrowded bus with tired overworked faces with uniforms now hanging in tatters or covered in grime and mud, search dogs looking more like unkempt mountain wolves than service dogs, sleeping figures hoping to catch a few minutes' rest before they arrived at the next job. Although I never said it, I was proud to be part of such a great adventure.

As we made our way to the incident, the sun was starting to set sending the sky into a fairy red glow that brought a comforting warmth on my face. We drove along the harbour road. It was easy to see how this place could become a great tourist destination, the sea was blue and the landscape was impressive if not somewhat bare due to deforestation, the climate was great for the sun worshipping tourist and the old world charm left over from French colonial occupation could be found on every street corner. Pity it was in such a poor state, I thought.

When we arrived at the Caribbean market, it was plain to see that this had been a big complex prior to the quake, reminding me of a large Walmart store in the UK. It was about three storeys high but was now no more than one storey, as the other two had collapsed inside the lower ones, an impressive sight to say the least. This was going to be a tough job for Echo and I now questioned if the dog that was only 75% fit could handle this type of environment.

The team set up in what was once the yard and main loading/unloading area at the rear of the store. As a reconnaissance was to take place prior to the teams going in, I decided to take Echo somewhere quiet and have a rest. I was soon joined by a few others who had sprawled out in the early evening cool air and fell asleep. It was dark when the word came back to start search ops and it was evident by looking at the building that several other teams had searched this complex in the days before our arrival. As a team completes a search, they draw certain markings on a building to tell follow-up teams what they have done or found, etc. It was decided that Echo would be deployed into a triangular breach (hole) cut into a concrete wall that had been made before our arrival. I was then to push Echo up a series of corridors ending up in what was described to me as a large void area. The brief was vague to say the least, but I nodded and told Echo we would be ok once we got going. Health and Safety did not really exist while on operations abroad and I was still amazed that no firefighters had been killed over the previous years. I prepared Echo and worked out a plan in case something went wrong. Always have a plan B. For example, what if Echo panicked in the confined space? What if I did? I thought back to the day in the tunnels when I said we would never do another confined space search. All these thoughts went through my head. On my command, Echo leapt through the triangle-shaped breach and we set off on our search. My first impression of the interior of this building left me feeling nervous. It was dark with the familiar but overwhelming smell of death nearby and the corridor I had been told to go down had collapsed, so I had to lay flat on my stomach and do a form of seal crawl to get down it with Echo in front of me. My head torch was next to useless in the dark and dust and gave off little light. During Echo's passage through the corridor, I could hear him whimpering and occasionally he would look back at me for reassurance. He was struggling to negotiate the mass of tangled shopping trolleys and fallen rubble, looking for the best way through. I could also feel that we were not alone and that 1,000 eyes were staring at me as I crawled. I was starting to get a bit panicky and the air was hard to breathe. My eyes were stinging with the grit and the sweat was mixing it into a concrete paste that made it difficult to see. I located two dead bodies as I went along and had to crawl over them at one point. They had been crushed flat by the impact of the ceiling falling on them and didn't make a pretty sight. Echo ignored them for the most part, but I could sense he was as uneasy as me. Every few feet a hand or other body part was sticking out of the rubble, I saw a young girl about 8 years old, both legs crushed flat, her eyes wide open as if she had looked death straight in the face in her last moments. After about 15 minutes, we reached an area where we could stand up. By this stage, I was covered in dust and what appeared to be purple dye but was in reality blood from the body I had crawled over earlier. Echo was also looking a sorry state as well; the blood and dust had gelled into a paste that was going to be tough to get off his coat and he was panting heavily. He looked uneasy and confused and from what I could see of his eyes they looked empty and somewhat dazed. As we moved along, we came across a group of our rescue team who had pitched a ladder to an upper floor area to gain access to it. I was asked if Echo could be carried up to see if any live scent could be detected on what remained of that area of the building. I agreed, but as no lifting harnesses were available, I would have to carry Echo up the ladder. Now, Echo was a 30kg Labrador and not easy to lift. As I picked him up, I regretted that I had not trained a Springer or some other light weight dog breed. He seemed to weigh a ton and it was difficult to climb the ladder with him. He had lost a lot of weight through dehydration, but in my weakened state he seemed heavier. I put him across my arms and used my body to hold him tight into the metal ladder, but I knew this was going to be a trauma. All was going well until we got halfway up the ladder, about 20ft up. Echo suddenly started to panic and fight me, he wanted to get out of this situation and fast. I thrust my body as tightly as I could against the ladder trying to trap Echo in a sort of vice between the two of us. It was no good, he was just too damn strong, and I knew that he was going to win this fight. We were about 20ft off the ground, I knew the fall would be the end of him. I held on as long as I could, but it was no good, my strength gave out. I decided that if he went, I was going with him. Maybe I could break his fall with my body, maybe I could take the sting out of it all if he landed on me. All this went through my mind in about five seconds. As the ladder started to shake, I decided to take the fall with him. Damn it, I thought, everybody dies at some point! Just as I started to release my grip on him and make ready for our descent, I heard a shout from behind me. One of our rescue team had heard the commotion and had seen what was going on. He ran to assist me and climed up the ladder shouting at me to keep hold of him. "Don't let him go," he screamed. As he came up behind me on the ladder, he wrapped his arms around me and Echo forcing us closer to the ladder and trapping us ensuring that no matter how hard Echo fought he was not going to break free. I was now squeezed like a lemon between the rescue guy and the dog. He told me to start slowly moving down the ladder while keeping a tight grip of the dog. I did as he said and, although it seemed to take forever, we were soon back on the ground, both very shaken. I thanked the guy who had put his own safety at risk for us. It was a most heroic thing to do, and a great example of what being a firefighter is all about. It was, however, the last straw for me and Echo and I cursed the day my request for a £56 lift harness had been refused by the Fire Service, £56 out of a multimillion-pound budget! The word "unbelievable" came to mind, as I reflected on my near-death experience.

The ladder experience had left me shaken, to say the least. I was no longer happy in this situation and I felt closed in by the smell and the congestion I was experiencing. I was dwelling on past traumatic experiences in India and Pakistan and wanted to get home as soon as I could. Dying here filled me with dread, I wanted to see Daniel again and forget this had ever happened. To be honest, I was going mad with worry and my anxiety was starting to boil over.

It was decided that the UK team had done enough at the market search. With no casualties located, the light had now turned to darkness and it was not safe to be walking around this unstable building in such circumstances. It was time to board the bus and head back to the Boo.

As we left the Caribbean market search, I knew that the deployment was coming to an end. I had had enough to be honest, the heat, the death and destruction, not to mention the madness of the situation, had left me empty and feeling isolated. I retired to my tent that evening and knew that my time in the overseas response team was coming to a close. I had been involved since 1993 and been on several high-profile incidents. I had been part of the five-man team who had carried out the first UK Fire Service overseas rescue when we lifted the boy and his mum out of the flats in India. I had seen the Himalayan snowline while in Pakistan and walked on the Khyber Pass. I had fulfilled my ambition to take a dog overseas and work him in the most hostile environments available; in short, I had done it all. Why risk anymore? I knew it was a matter of time before someone died in this environment. As I said earlier, health and safety didn't apply abroad as it did in the UK, the situations described in this chapter pay testament to that. I felt that someone was going to pay a high price at some point. As I drifted off to sleep, my thoughts turned to happier times. I smiled at the thought of seeing Echo playing in the fields near our home, seeing him splashing in the sea when we took him to the beach. Echo and the other search dogs had played a big part in this job and played it well. He had taken risks far beyond what was expected of a Fire Service search dog on operations. I was proud of him and his achievements. As I took my last breath before the sleep rolled in, I thought of Daniel and my fantastic wife, Sue.

Echo as a young chap.

Echo in full PPE

Echo indicating on body during a training exercise

Caribbean market search site
Note markings from other international search teams.
Echo's entry point was slightly left of centre.

Echo proudly wearing his PDSA Order of Merit medal

Pride of Britain

Ace in his search harness

Echo in his uniform

Photo courtesy of Bernard Ashton

Chapter 5

MAYHEM

On my return from the Haiti job, Echo had been taken into quarantine for six months because of UK law. The media circus when we landed at Manchester Airport was expected, but unwelcome, as I was not feeling 100%. Echo had been taken off me at Gatwick airport and whisked away into captivity before the North West Fire Service teams caught a connecting flight to Manchester. When we entered the airport terminal we were met by reporters, all asking the same questions: How was Echo and how did he perform in Haiti? Had he recovered from his ordeal and what my thoughts were about him going into quarantine? We were quickly directed to a small room where our families were waiting. It was great to see Daniel and Sue and I felt the world had been lifted off my shoulders, even for a short time.

As the days after my return passed, I found myself in an ever-increasing state of shock that I couldn't shake off. We, as a team, had not had any decompression to allow us to blow off steam and I was having real problems pressing the reset button, so to speak. I was hyper vigilant, and any sudden sound or unexpected event sent me into meltdown. I had become a different person that I couldn't seem to connect with. It was as if I was looking at myself through another person's eyes and I didn't like the feeling at all. As it turned out, this would shape my life for the years to come.

Echo had been sent to a quarantine facility in the Blackpool area, about an hour's drive from my home. It was small but looked like a place Echo would be looked after. He was left in a small concrete-bottomed cage that looked out on to a central courtyard. It was small but had everything he needed. It broke my heart seeing him incarcerated in such a small place but that was the deal. I used to visit him weekly, but when I was leaving, he howled, and I had to cover my ears as it drove me mad listening to him. Sue and Daniel never came with me on my visits as they couldn't take seeing him boxed in. I was fearful Echo was starting to stress out at the lack of stimulation as he paced up and down his room like a crazed lion. I had a chat with the kennel manager, and he suggested putting some chickens in the courtyard to wander about. This would give Echo something to look at and focus on. The chickens arrived and it had an immediate effect on him. He just sat with his nose pressed up against the cage staring intently at them. It was his new pastime and he seemed to love it, but I did fear what may happen if ever he got to within striking distance of these chickens.

The six months of Echo's quarantine passed surprisingly quickly. The physical scars of Haiti had healed but the mental ones I wasn't sure about. Visiting him combined with my work schedule, made the time pass quickly. It was a warm July day in 2010 when he was released. I drove up to the kennels in Blackpool, which had been his prison for the last few months and when I arrived, I was told he was ready in the yard for collection. I said I hoped the chickens were ok. As I made my way to the rear of the building, I could hear him barking almost begging me to collect him and take him for a good run. When he saw me, he went mad, spinning around several times then running at me at full speed, jumping up and head butting me nearly knocking me flying. He had put on some weight during his time in captivity, but it didn't stop him trying to jump over the top of me. After thanking the kennel staff and chickens for looking after him, I loaded him into my service dog van and took him home. To say he was glad to get home was an understatement. Sue was waiting for him at the front of our house and as I let him out of the van, he ran straight past her and into the house frantically. He ran round for about 15 minutes knocking ornaments and lamps over as he went, until he finally calmed down and allowed Sue to give him a good hug. One thing had become apparent during these 15 minutes of madness, Echo was now an overweight and out of condition boy, who would need considerable time invested in him in fitness and diet before I could even think about re-addressing his search training.

In the weeks that followed I brought Echo up to an acceptable standard of fitness. He lost some weight and was again able to keep up with me on my mountain bike. His search training went well and assisted by Daniel, I brought Echo back to full search readiness. This had not been without incident though. One day, while training near a local farm, I was directing Echo to a casualty, when, out of the blue, two chickens walked into the search area. Oh my God, were my first thoughts on seeing the two birds just minding their own business. Echo immediately locked on to them and, with evil intent in his eyes he bolted at full speed towards the two now fleeing birds. I could imagine him saying, it's payback time for all the teasing in the kennels. The two birds tried to get away, but this new, fitter Echo was too fast for them. At a full sprint, he scooped one of them up and flung it in the air, the second one made good its escape, but the other was not so lucky. As it hit the ground Echo prepared to go in for the kill, but luckily, he had ideas of teasing it the way they had teased him in his kennel. He pawed it a few times and pushed it around, but it was still fighting hard and they disappeared in a mist of feathers. This gave me just enough time to reach Echo as he was about to deal the death blow to this now struggling bird. I grabbed his head and pulled him away while gathering the chicken in my other hand. I now had a mad Labrador in one hand and a crazy chicken in the other. It was a bizarre sight to see and one which I was struggling to get out of. In the end, I decided to drop the chicken and just hold on to Echo, and as the chicken hit the ground it must have seen its opportunity to flee and in no time it was off and running hard for home, a relief to say the least. As it turned out my fears about

Echo's loss of performance while incarcerated were unfounded. He was alert and, dare I say it, even better than before he went into quarantine.

On 10th August 2010, I declared that Echo the hero dog of Haiti was "back on the run" and ready for action.

The 15th October 2010 started as a slow day. I was out walking Echo along with my other search dog, Lucy, around 7am and taking our usual route along the river and through the woods. This was my favourite time to walk the dogs as it was so quiet with no one else around. I always used it as a time to reflect on past events, but on this day, the quietness was disturbed by the sound of a dull thud in the far distance. I stopped momentarily and thought that this was a most unusual sound and one that I had not heard before. I listened for a few seconds more but heard nothing so carried on with my walk. After about 15 minutes, I reached my dog van and after loading the dogs I decided to check my service phone that I had left in the van, as I was off duty this day. I noticed a text message had come through and as I opened it a chill ran down my spine and my heart rate increased considerably, "On Call USAR Team to Respond to Collapsed Building". I immediately contacted the Manchester Fire Service control and asked what the incident was. I spoke to a young operator who excitedly informed me that a row of houses in the Irlam area of Manchester had suddenly exploded and there were reports of a young child trapped in the rubble. Her voice was strained with a hint of panic. I asked her why a dog had not been mobilised, but she seemed too distracted to give me an answer and I decided immediately that this was a job for Echo; with a child's life in the balance I could not wait to be officially mobilised, so I told the young operator that the dog was going to respond to this incident immediately.

As I set off, I turned on all my blue lights, as well as listening to updates of the incident from fire control. I also tuned into a local radio station for info on developments and the latest traffic news around the job. It was now 7.30ish on a weekday and the traffic was heavy and at a standstill in most places. As I made my way through the gridlock, it became apparent from what info I could glean from the radio that this was a serious incident, possibly a gas explosion that had left several houses destroyed. I contacted fire control again and asked if the Lancashire Fire Service search dog had been mobilised, as I knew Echo would need support for a job of this size.

Lancashire's search dog was called Isle, a dainty Collie who was run by a pal of mine called Kurt. He was an ex-Royal Marine and an ardent fitness fanatic who had become a good friend over the previous few years due to our almost constant dog training events. He had been in the Fire Service about 20 years and was an experienced handler. I was pleased he was attending the incident to support and assist us.

When I arrived, I was met by a scene of chaos. I could see what remained of a semi-detached house, people and firefighters were running around all over the place and it seemed that no real order had been established. Three fire engines had arrived a few minutes before me and I could see the officer in charge frantically trying to gain the upper hand in this chaotic situation. The early stages of any incident like this are confusing and demanding for everyone.

I located the incident commander to tell him the dog unit had arrived and that I would await further instructions after the situation had been brought under some form of control. He told me that we would be required but to give him five minutes to get a grip of people. I took this opportunity to let Echo have a leg stretch and, after a short while, I was approached by a Group Manager, a form of middle manager in the Fire Service, who wanted me to undertake a search with the dog to establish if anyone was missing. It had still not been verified that all people in the house had been accounted for and the idea of a child missing was still floating around. By this time, Kurt and his dog Isle had turned up from Lancashire Fire Service. It was good to see him and I felt the pressure lifted off me a bit, and to be able to consult with him as to the best way to carry out the search was a big help. After a short conversation with Kurt and, with a sense of urgency in our actions, we decided to use Echo and back up his search with Isle. I got Echo from the van. He was definitely ready to work, as the van was bouncing up and down because of his enthusiasm. As I returned to the search site, I could feel 100 pairs of eyes staring at me as the incident ground had come to a standstill while the dog search was carried out. Momentarily, I was taken back to Haiti and the large crowds that gathered during many of the dog searches. Kurt was spotting for me to make sure I didn't miss any potential voids where people may be trapped, which in turn allowed me to focus 100% on the dog. I ensured all the other firefighters had left the rubble pile, so the dog didn't get too distracted by the presence of other people. This is a lesson I had learned years before after an incident down south when firefighters had caused the dogs to be distracted while searching. Echo was the hero dog of Haiti and had to live up to his reputation, so the less distractions the better. As I took him to the edge of this now destroyed house, I scanned the scene in front of me. I could see upturned furniture and clothes that had been blown out of wardrobes, but my biggest concern was the amount of wood that had been damaged in the blast and was now a potential hazard for Echo. I left off his search harness as I didn't want it getting snagged and causing me more issues than I already had. I selected a place to start the search based on the wind direction and set him off. He worked his way to the top of what remained of the house, then down the middle. The going was very tough with twisted metal and large pieces of debris to contend with. I could see he was struggling to make headway through this tangled mess that was once a house, and finding stable ground for his feet. He could not move more than a few feet without having to clamber over some obstruction or hazard. His eyes were darting from side to side and his nose was fixed firmly on the debris pile. If a child was missing, this dog was going to find it. I could see blood on Echo's nose and knew he has sustained an injury, but moderation and pain were two things this dog didn't acknowledge. As he went on, I gave Kurt the nod to get his dog ready as Echo was getting tired. The vast majority of the rubble pile was searched by Echo and it was now up to Kurt to finish the job and deploy Isle to confirm what Echo had already told us. Dogs are not perfect and can make mistakes, so we deploy two to make sure we leave no-one trapped in the rubble. Echo finished his part in the job with a search around the perimeter to see if anyone had been blown clear of the house by the blast. We had seen that happen before, but as it turned out Echo did his job and did it well, apart from eating what remained of a pack of butter from a fridge that had burst open. He had searched for about 20 minutes, which was enough to cover a rubble pile of this size and gave no indications of trapped people. That was enough for me to say that the pile was clear with no-one trapped inside. Kurt and Isle confirmed this with the follow-up search with Isle struggling just as much as Echo over the rough ground. Isle always made me smile, she was the direct opposite of Echo, small and dainty with a tendency to move slowly over the search sites. Echo, on the other hand, was a bull in a china shop and most of his injuries were self-inflicted due to the speed he moved. The dogs did a couple more of what we call 'confirmation searches' as is normal in this type of incident, just to 'confirm' no-one was trapped, but, as expected, no people were located by the dogs and it was declared that the rubble pile was clear of casualties. As it turned out the 'missing 'child was located with her mother sometime later, to everyone's relief. When the last fire engine had been stood down, I gave Echo one last run with Isle while I chatted to

Kurt about how the job had gone, a sort of debrief. We then made our way home, tired but satisfied we had done our best. This incident was a great example of why a service with such a high profile as Manchester Fire Service should have a search and rescue dog capability and it was a great testament to the training and assessment process Echo had been through.

A short time after this job, I was sat at work when I received a telephone call from the reception downstairs. They said a very large cardboard box had arrived for me and was in reception and could I move it as soon as possible. I went down to see what this mysterious package was. It had mine and Echo's name written on the front in large writing. I managed to get the box upstairs to my office and after looking at it for a few minutes I got the scissors and cut along the top to open it. By this time, a crowd had gathered, and as I cut it open and peered inside, I could see a note. It read, "Just to say thank you to Mike and Echo for helping at the Irlam explosion". It was from a local pet shop and was full of dog toys and treats, far too many really, but it was a fantastic gesture and made me very proud to have contributed in some small way to the outcome. Echo was a happy dog when he got them.

Two weeks later, I and the other members of the team that had been to Haiti, received calls to inform us that due to our efforts in Haiti we were to be invited to London to receive the Pride of Britain award. This was a big surprise and a great honour for the individuals and Manchester Fire Service. I was told that Echo would not be required, which was a great relief as a manic Labrador was the last thing you needed while trying to remain calm and focused on the TV. When I told Sue, she was understandably excited and started looking for an evening dress for the occasion. I was sorted; I just borrowed my dad's old dinner suit. All the arrangements were made via the programme makers and tickets and schedules were issued to the individuals attending. We were told that we were to be in London for two days and would be staying in a top hotel next to the river. "What river?" Sue asked. A visit to 10 Downing Street was also planned to meet David Cameron and we were to be introduced to a host of celebrities including the fantastic Carol Vorderman. Now, that brought a big smile to my face as I really fancied her. This all sounded fantastic until a few days before we were due to depart via train from Manchester.

As I was driving to the gym on a rainy Thursday morning, my in-car phone rang. I answered and a voice said that they worked for Pride of Britain and were calling to ask if I would consider bringing Echo to London to take part in the event and to meet everyone involved. I was stunned at this request because Echo was not the easiest dog to control at the best of times and trying to keep him occupied for two days in the confines of London away from the rolling fields where we lived was going to be awkward. I reluctantly agreed, as it would add the aww factor to the proceedings and raise the profile of dogs in the Fire Service that was desperately needed. I told Sue that we would have company on the train, and she was not impressed to say the least.

The day of departure arrived. We met at the train station and were told that we would be travelling first class courtesy of Virgin Trains. We all had our bags, dinner suits and evening dresses, but as well, Sue and I had this manic, moulting Labrador who despite my efforts to tire him out prior to the journey, was still like a dog possessed. On boarding the train, I sat Echo between myself and Sue and he somehow managed to squeeze himself under the chair I was sat on. I hoped he would remain there for the duration of the journey, but I could sense trouble was brewing. As we set off, my boss, Gary, suggested we all have a drink to celebrate the coming event and to settle the nerves a bit, but to be honest, the wine and beer flowed a bit too easily and after about an hour I nodded off in my chair. When I woke, we were well down south and, as I looked over, I noticed that Sue had also nodded off. But, when I put my hand under the chair expecting to feel a hairy Lab, I was met by an empty space with just a few old blond dog hairs where my hero search dog used to be. I immediately woke Sue and asked her why she had gone to sleep and left Echo unattended. I had to blame someone, so she seemed the natural choice. She immediately came back with some form of sarcastic remark and, as a result, a domestic row broke out as to who was to blame for Echo going missing. After we had agreed that it was Sue's fault (I agreed… not Sue) we set off in hunt for this elusive dog and the first place I looked through was the bar car. I knew the lure of bacon butties would be too much for him to resist, but as it turned out no one in the carriage had seen him. We looked in the toilets and everywhere you can imagine a dog could hide on a train. I was now becoming worried and the initial annoyance at his disappearance was now turning into panic. I decided that if ever they made 'Echo the Movie', I would leave this part out. But, as I was about to give up and go back to my seat, I noticed in the far distance a young girl sat alone. I could just see the top of her head. I could also see what looked like a dog's tail sticking out from the empty seat next to her and, as I approached, I was hoping that this was Echo and not some Guide Dog for the Blind that this girl owned. As I got closer, I could see the girl reading a book so immediately assumed that she was not blind. As I got level with her it became obvious that this was no Guide Dog for the Blind but Echo who, by the girl's account, had wandered up the carriage about an hour previously and jumped on the seat next to her and laid his head on her lap and gone to sleep, just as on the plane to Haiti, when he did the same with the young hostess. The relief at finding him was immense and as I tried to apologise to this girl, she stopped me and said that it was no problem at all, and she had enjoyed his company. I explained to her who he was and what we were going to London for and she asked if she could take a selfie with him to show her mum. I was getting a real sense of how people now felt about Echo and that they wanted to be associated with him and his story. I, of course, agreed to this selfie. When we arrived in London, we were met by a representative from the Pride of Britain programme who accompanied us to our hotel. On entering our room, we found a hospitality pack on the bed consisting of champagne and other goodies and a large dog bed on the floor together with a bag of dog treats for Echo, which he wasted no time getting stuck into. It was luxury to say the least and we felt excited at the thought of what was to come next. We were told to be ready for an early evening dinner with Carol Vorderman, who would go through the following day's proceedings and what to expect once the event got going. As I expected, she was as gorgeous in real life as on the TV. I started to tell her a joke about a dyslexic Welshman when Sue told me to be quiet and not show her up.

After a good night's sleep and a good chat with the other winners, we were picked up at the hotel by coach and taken on a sightseeing tour of London. This was a welcome excursion, as Sue had never been to our nation's capital before. We were shown all the sights and I was surprised just how busy the capital was. The tour terminated at 10 Downing Street for a lunch date with the PM, David Cameron. This was to be my third visit to Downing Street having been twice before after the quakes in India and Pakistan. Sue thought it was exciting, but Echo and I just took it all in our stride.

As we entered through the big black doors of Downing Street, we were accompanied upstairs where a light lunch was provided along with a glass of wine. Echo was on his best behaviour, for once, but was eyeing the buffet for any scraps that were to fall his way. When the PM finally came in, he came to each of us individually and asked about our experiences in Haiti. He made a big fuss over Echo and had his picture taken with him. As he was asking about Echo and his contribution to the quake effort. I asked if there was anywhere that I could take

Echo to allow him to stretch his legs and have a wee. He summoned one of his security staff and told them to escort me and the dog to the Downing Street gardens and to wait until Echo had done what he had to. As we entered the gardens via a large security door, I released Echo who was by this time bursting, as he charged round the gardens glad to be free of his collar and lead. I passed the time chatting to the security guard and basking in the autumn sun. He asked about Echo's work and seemed genuinely interested in his efforts in Haiti, but as we were talking, I heard a loud disturbing scream coming from the direction of an overgrown bush in the middle of this large garden complex. I, and the now nervous security guard, ran over to where the scream had come from. Had Echo discovered some intruders trying to break into Downing Street and foiled the crime adding to his already escalating fame? As we peered into the bush, we noticed a man who it turned out was a gardener just tidying up the leaves. He was flat on his back with Echo towering over him almost pinning him to the ground. I quickly restrained Echo and asked if this now shaking gardener was ok. As he got to his feet, he brushed himself down and said that in 20 years of working at Downing Street he had never seen a dog in the gardens and it was the last thing he was expecting, let alone it pinning him to the floor and holding him hostage. In the end, he saw the funny side of it and allowed Echo to roam the gardens freely, exploring every corner of this famous building.

The evening of the event arrived; it was a red-carpet arrival with lots of press and fans of the attending stars shouting out their names. As we all got off the coach, it was nice to see that people knew who Echo was and we were stopped several times to have our photos taken. We were escorted into the building and shown to our table. Each table had several celebrities on it, and we got to sit next to Sheridan Smith, who, it turned out, was fantastic and fell in love with Echo immediately. We also had

Jason Donovan and many other well-known faces within touching distance. After the initial introductions, we settled down for a gala dinner followed by the presentations. This seemed to take forever, and the Manchester fire team were up last. As the evening wore on, Echo became more restless and started to play up by barking and being a general pain in the ass. He took a dislike to the overhead cameras and every time they hovered over him, he tried to attack them. He even managed to break into Sheridan Smith's handbag and destroy all her make up by eating it. But she seemed to see the funny side of it when she discovered the contents of her bag all over the floor. As our turn arrived, a short video was shown of our time in Haiti that made the hair on the back on my neck stand up. The thoughts and memories came flooding back and I found myself transported to a time that I had fought very hard to forget. When we were called up on stage the whole room stood up to applaud us, which was most unnerving. We were lined up with Echo near the middle of the group and asked some questions about our work during the earthquake. They kept saying what heroes we were which made the team feel uncomfortable. Hero is a strong word and not to be used lightly. Then, just as the award was being presented, the young girl that the Manchester team had rescued in Haiti surprisingly appeared on the stage with her mother. It was a nice ending to an evening that was a great success.

After the presentations we mingled with the stars, we met too many to mention but Sue's highlight was meeting West Life and Jason Donovan. I had a meaningful talk with Jason, and we agreed that there were definitely 'too many broken hearts in the world'. I spoke at length with Simon Cowell about dogs and he seemed very interested in how Echo did his job. But with all the glamour of the evening, my personal highlight was meeting an excellent group of WW2 fighter pilots who had served in the Battle of Britain, who spoke of exploits shooting down enemy planes and general heroics of the period and how they had used Labradors like Echo as squadron mascots during the summer of 1940. They regaled a story about how a squadron Labrador had been killed during an air raid when the "buggers dropped a bomb on it", as they put it. One pilot gave me his Battle of Britain lapel pin that I will forever cherish. It was a great privilege to meet them. As the evening wore on, I became more restless and could see Echo was getting fed up with being patted and stroked, so we decided to get a taxi back to our hotel and have some quiet time. We put Echo to bed and went down for a last drink. We smiled at what we had just been through and told each other that it was a once-in-a-lifetime event. As I stared into my glass of white wine I could still hear a thousand screams, a thousand faces, begging me to search their homes with Echo, pulling me to where they wanted me to go, screaming at me to do something to help. The people of Haiti had got into my head and I knew that at some point I would have to return to put my demons to rest. Although I had not been diagnosed with PTSD at that point, I knew that I was not a well man. It was a horrible feeling and haunted me for years to come.

The next morning, as well as nursing hangovers, we had to make the long journey back to Manchester on the train. To be honest, by this time I had had enough of the glamour and the high life and just wanted to go home and put my feet up. Echo was becoming increasingly restless and Sue was totally knackered from all the excitement. As we were approaching Manchester, Gary, our boss, informed us that we would be required on local TV that evening for an interview by the presenters. It was the last thing I needed!

The experience had been good and looking back on Haiti and the Pride of Britain it was obvious that it had been an incredible experience for most of the team, as many of them would never get the chance to deploy overseas again, but for me it was becoming a common occurrence. I had done my bit and I felt it was time to hand over to younger, fitter hands.

CHAPTER 6

FLASHBACKS

After all the fuss of the previous few months was over, I was glad that it was just me and my dogs again. No more press cameras trying for the perfect shot or newspapers asking the same old questions about Haiti and the Pride of Britain etc. It was just me and Echo, along with his side kick, Lucy, my fire investigation dog. I enjoyed this time and spent as much of it as I could training the two dogs to keep them sharp and ready for action. I never mentioned it to anyone, but I could see the earthquake in Haiti and the subsequent quarantine had taken its toll on Echo and he was now looking old and worn out. I was like most dog owners and in some denial about Echo getting old and could not imagine a time when he was not with me.

The pace of our working days remained the same, with Lucy being the busiest dog due to the high demand from the police for her specialist skills and the now ritual round of school visits that seem to haunt me. Everyone wanted to meet Echo and hear about his stories and adventures. The pupils at schools I was visiting even took to making life size models of Echo to present to me when I arrived to give a talk. It was all very thoughtful but wore on the nerves after a while. It was around this time that I started to experience flashbacks, almost instant recollection of sights and sounds. One day, while talking to a class about Echo, I looked over and saw a large picture someone had drawn of Echo. I was sure it would be presented to me at the end of the event. The picture, drawn with childlike innocence, depicted Echo carrying a small child to safety in his mouth. It was more than I could stand, and I started to well up as my voice broke into a faint whisper as my mind was taken back to the school in Haiti, and all the dead children. It was just one example of the roller coaster of emotions everyday life was throwing at me.

Although I was busy with what I considered mundane activities, I longed for some more action for Echo and to again, test him in a real-life situation. Search and rescue dogs in the Fire Service do not receive many call-outs due to the nature of the work they do. If Echo got three callouts in a year that was considered busy, if you compare that to the 70 or 80 call-outs Lucy received in the same period Echo was almost dormant. So, we trained and trained travelling up and down the country on various events. Around this time, I had a new helper arrive in the form of a firefighter called Clare. She was a member of the Manchester Fire Service Urban Search and Rescue unit and was keen to get involved in training the dog team. I was pleased that she had come forward to get involved, as my son Daniel, who had been my right-hand man over the previous four years had now discovered girls and didn't want to be bothered coming out with me training, when he was much happier chasing the ladies.

Clare was about 39 when she approached me to get involved. She was tall and athletic in her build and had a smile and personality that I instantly took to. She was very enthusiastic and harbored a desire to train her own dog one day. We got together and she met the dogs, who took to her immediately and, after a short while, she was hooked, and enquired when we could train again. I knew she would be a great asset in the future and, as it turned out, a good friend when things started to unravel for me.

In March of 2011, I was informed that Echo had been nominated for an award at Crufts and was entered into the Friends for Life competition. This was more good news and another opportunity for Echo to add to his ever-increasing list of awards. He was to go up against several other working dogs to be voted on by the public to see who would win, including a police dog and varying types of assistance dogs. We had to take part in a short film about Echo and his exploits in Haiti, to demonstrate Echo's abilities to the viewing public and give them an idea on what they would be voting for. I knew it was important to get the message across during this film that Echo was a hero dog, and the one to vote for. Clare, as always, was enthusiastic to get involved and when the day came to film, she played the part of the body so we could demonstrate Echo's search ability to the viewing public. I had to do a piece to camera and explain who Echo was and what he did. I think you can still view this on You Tube if you look hard enough. Echo performed very well and gave a good demonstration, even if it did require three takes!

The day of the competition came, and the winner was to be announced in the main arena at the NEC in Birmingham during the Crufts event. The Kennel Club had arranged for a hotel room the evening before the event to make it a special occasion. We also had a free bar, as well as food in the extensive hotel restaurant. It was set to be a great evening before the event, until my phone rang. Daniel was at home looking after Lucy and he had called me to say he could smell what he thought was gas in the house. I asked if he was sure it was gas and to make certain before we took any action. I knew, at that point, that Sue would not rest until she knew, and we were going to be heading home soon. Daniel was sure it was gas, so I told him that we were on our way and to open every window in the house. I was annoyed, to say the least. We had a free room, and a free bar that we were not going to taking advantage of. It was 100 miles to our home in Manchester and it seemed to take a lifetime to get there. When I opened the front door of the house Sue rushed in behind me to see if Daniel was ok. I immediately recognized the smell and knew that it wasn't gas. It was a sweet smell that reminded me of my youth. As I hunted around the house for this illusive smell, I made my way upstairs to the airing cupboard that we used to dry towels, and, when I opened the door, the smell was strong and childhood memories of building Airfix model aircraft came flooding back. As I moved the top layer of towels,

I could see a half-made model Spitfire aircraft that I had started a few weeks before and not completed. As I opened the box, I could see that the tube of glue used to hold the model together had leaked thus causing the offending smell. I called Daniel and Sue upstairs and told them what had caused the smell. I told Daniel that he had done the right thing phoning us, as it was not clear to him what it was at that point. As it was late, I decided that we would spend the night at home and travel back to the event very early the next morning. I was gutted; I had visions of drinking free cocktails and eating off an extravagant menu while retelling stories of Echo's heroic deeds overseas to eager ears. Instead, I had a bowl of cornflakes and went to bed!

The next morning, we got up extra early and loaded Echo into the car. We set off for Birmingham full of anticipation for the impending results of the competition Echo was entered in. I parked up and we made our way into the main part of the Crufts arena. The results were not going to be announced until the early evening, so we took the opportunity to look round and see what we could buy for the dogs. We were stopped constantly by people who had voted for Echo to win and they wished us good luck. Again, I found myself recalling the story of Echo and his exploits overseas. The day was long and tiring and by 5pm I had had enough and just wanted to get on with it.

When the time came to announce the results, the dogs entered in the competition were marched one by one into the main arena. As we walked on, a loudspeaker announced who we were and what exploits we had undertaken to get us nominated. I felt embarrassed and a little bit vulnerable with all these eyes upon me. Lots of people stood up to applaud Echo, but was I doing the right thing off the back of so much tragedy and pain? I played along with the show. When all the dogs were in a long line the presenter, Clare Balding, came along and asked us a few questions. Echo did his usual trick and tried to attack the cameraman who came in just a bit too close for comfort. She asked me if I was proud of Echo and what sort of dog was he. I wanted to say he was a pain in the bum at times, but in the event said he was my best mate, and I was very proud of his achievements. Very diplomatic, I thought.

After all the questions had been asked, the lights dimmed, and the speaker announced the results and to raise the tension allowed a 10-second pause before he gave the verdict. To be honest, I was fully expecting Echo to win. No dog should have gone through the hell hole that was Haiti and not be given a lifetime achievement award.

After all the hype and build-up, the moment arrived. My throat was dry, and I had a nervous itch in my stomach as I whispered to Echo that he would smash this and take another cup home to Manchester. Then, after what seemed like an age, the announcer called the name of an assistance dog called Kaiser as the winner. Everyone clapped and, although I felt robbed, I knew that Kaiser was a hero in his own right, and it was a justifiable result. Echo was the runner-up so not all was lost. As we walked out of the arena, we said our congratulations to the winners and had some pictures taken as a group. By this time, I was really tired and longed for some rest. As we made our way to the car, the winner came up to me and said that she has been asked to go straight to London to appear on breakfast TV. When I heard this, I was glad to be a runner-up, a trip to London was the last thing I needed that night.

As we drove home, Sue was falling asleep and Echo had already crashed out on the back seat. I thought about what a crazy ride the last few years had been, from the initial idea of getting a dog, to the situation we were in now. Echo was now showing signs of his age, his blond hair was now turning white, and his eyes, once alert and sharp, were now drooping with a sort of sadness in them. The same could be said about me, injuries sustained years before were now haunting me as I got older and the clarity in my life that I had as a youth had now faded into a grey haze of uncertainty. I watched the lights of the motorway disappear one by one as I drove under them and wondered what the future would hold for Echo and me. Would we be remembered for our efforts or would we be consigned to history? As it turned out, the mighty Echo had one last award to win.

CHAPTER 7

NEW ROLE

It was now 2012 and the events of the previous two years were now a distant memory. Although Echo had managed to bag himself yet another award in the form of the International Fund for Animal Welfare, Animal of the Year 2011, this, combined with his Pride of Britain award, made him one of the most highly decorated dogs in the UK Fire Service. He received the IFAW award at the House of Lords in London. Lots of people came to see him and ask about his exploits, it was great fun, and we had a great day. The highlight of the trip was afternoon tea in the Members' restaurant and meeting Brian May, the lead guitarist with the band *Queen*. When we were introduced to Brian, he congratulated us on Echo's award and got down on his knees to have a play with him. Echo thought it was great and was loving all the attention. Sue, in her usual foot in mouth way, asked Brian if he was still playing with *Bon Jovi*. I took her to one side and said that if she had nothing sensible to say then say nothing at all. The award was presented and, after a tour around the House of Lords, we made our way back to the Union Jack Club where we were staying to have a celebration drink.

The two years had gone by quickly and Echo was now eight years old and showing signs of fatigue. He still bore the physical scars from his Haiti experience in the form of a damaged eye socket sustained falling out of the back of a US Army jeep at speed, and a scar on his head from the Caribbean market search. I still harboured the ones that left me mentally paralysed at times. Life had been fairly peaceful for us in the meantime. My relationship with Echo had changed though, I began to see him as my link to the past, my bridge to another time and place, when I was feeling low and depression was setting in. He was my window to some form of salvation, and I started to fear what life without him would be like.

In 2011, I acquired a replacement for Echo in the form of Ace, a one-year-old yellow Lab who came to the Fire Service by way of a donation. In 2012 Ace was still in training so could not be deployed operationally, he was, however, very enthusiastic and, to be honest, a bit manic about his searching. He was slender and toned for a Lab and had a chiselled physique; he looked the part. He also had a search drive that was fantastic, so I was pleased he came our way.

Echo had not seen much action over the previous two years, training with Clare and school visits had been the normal routine. He had learned a few tricks to amuse the kids during these visits, but it frustrated me that this search dog, who was at his prime, was being wasted teaching kids to test smoke alarms and keep safe around fire. I could see the sense in it, but it annoyed me just the same. I wanted action and wanted it there and then, I had an almost self-destruct attitude to see more and more collapsed buildings. My mind was all over the place with nightmares and long periods of my day lost somewhere in my mind, periods that I could not account for. Sue was supportive, but I only confided in Clare the true extent of my mental health. I had moved into the Fire Service headquarters as part of a fire investigation team review, as I had a fire investigation dog in the form of Lucy. I was attached for admin purposes to this department. I was now deskbound when not training or making school visits. I found this a strange place; I was in the Fire Service but found myself surrounded by civilians with almost made-up job titles. On one occasion, a civilian manager tried to assert their position on me by challenging the way I was dressed. As this person talked at me, I seemed to shut out all the noise coming from their mouth and just thought of the lift harness that these individuals had refused to buy for Echo before the Haiti job and how that decision nearly killed us both. I wondered how much we were paying this person to talk to me with such disrespect. As I never took these people seriously, I just smiled as they walked away.

Someone once told me to be careful what I wished for, well it's true! June 2012 had been a slow month for the dog team, with only one call-out for the fire investigation dog and Echo undertaking his usual round of educational visits. One day I was off work on a rest day. I was in the gym I had constructed at the bottom of my garden. It contained a running machine and a spin cycle as well as a selection of free weights, it was a place I liked to go to get away from the world and be alone with my thoughts. By this stage I had been diagnosed with PTSD by a mental health assessment organised by the Fire Service in Manchester and was working my way through some treatment. I decided to approach them when I could not hide the condition anymore and my mind was ready to explode, I was not in a good place at all mentally. I was just about to finish a tough session on my runner when I got a call from the deputy USAR team leader Neal Pilkington. He told me that an incident in the north of the county was developing and I should get Echo ready for action. I liked Neal as he had a sense of humour that was no longer PC enough for the modern Fire Service and, although well over retirement age, I liked to think he hung around to annoy the establishment. He loved what he did and had always been a big Echo supporter. From early reports, a row of houses had exploded, and it was reported that a child was missing in the rubble and others may also be unaccounted for. He asked if Echo was available to respond and how quickly I could be on the scene. I told him that I would turn out immediately and ran into the house and got my gear together. I decided that as well as taking Echo I would take Ace too as he was nearing the completion of his training and could be of some use. As I set off, I got an update from fire control as to the latest situation and then made my way on to the M60 towards the incident. Driving along, I felt nervous and almost claustrophobic at the thought of seeing what I knew was coming my way. I told myself this was just another job, so I needed to get a grip. As I was coming off at the junction that would take me to the job, I noticed in the distance the USAR vehicles from Lancashire Fire Service that had also been called. I saw that they had a police escort so, not knowing the exact location of the incident, I decided to tag on to the rear of the convoy. After about 10 minutes of travelling along the small, congested A roads, we made a left turn into the incident cordon area about 400 metres from the explosion. As I parked up, I could clearly see the devastation in front of me, it looked like several houses had been destroyed with debris spread over a large area and I could see a police officer covered in dust who had obviously attempted some sort of rescue but was now walking about in a form of dazed shock. I had seen this look on people's faces before, I said to myself. People were running all over the place and I could see a woman crying in the distance. It was an all too familiar sight for me and I braced myself for the task ahead.

After the initial shock of what I witnessed on arrival, I made my way to the Fire Service command unit to book in and tell them that the dog was available if needed. A friend of mine, who I had served with whilst a firefighter at Salford, greeted me as I entered the command vehicle, but gestured to me to keep quiet as a briefing was taking place between some of the senior fire and police officers. As usual, they talked at length about various methods of searching the building, but never once did I hear a mention of the dog playing its part. I smiled and wondered how these individuals with zero experience in search and rescue on this scale could possibly put together a search strategy, but who was I to question the system. After the briefing, I approached my friend and told him the dog unit was ready to deploy.

After what seemed an age of waiting around, I noticed a group of Fire Service search technician's approaching the scene, specialists from our technical response team. These guys knew the score and I knew the job had just taken a turn for the better. I enquired as to what they were going to do, and they told me that they were going to undertake a Delsar sweep to see if they could locate anyone. A Delsar is an item of very sensitive listening equipment that the Fire Service use to detect sound in a collapsed structure, but it has limitations, the main one being a human must use it.

As I watched them set up the equipment, I suggested to the team leader that we use the dog, as he was sat in his car kennel with his paw up his ass and doing no good at all. I told them that Echo could be deployed immediately and be working while they were still figuring out how to set up the gear. I suspected they had not thought of using the dog at this stage, but they said it was a good idea and to go and get him ready, so after taking Echo on a short walk to allow him to have a pee and stretch his legs, I put on his protective boots and made my way to where the search was to start. As I walked towards the incident, I could see that the explosion had destroyed several terraced houses and left a large gap where two houses once stood. This gap revealed a lot of twisted metal and large pieces of broken wood and debris and a very difficult search was in store for Echo. More worrying was that a small child was dead and still in the rubble that was once his home. It was a heart-breaking thought, but, unfortunately for me, a familiar one. Before starting the search, I got on the radio and requested the assistance of another search dog as back-up to Echo which came in the form of a New Dimensions-trained Springer Spaniel from a neighbouring Fire Service.

When I was ready to start the search, I informed the other firefighters to move out of the way and allow Echo space to move freely on the rubble. I could see that he had already scented the dead child and was looking over to where we knew he was buried. As I let him off his lead and gave him the "away find" command Echo immediately turned to his right and ran at full speed to where the child was buried. A large piece of roofing was covering a mattress under which the small child was lying dead. As Echo approached it, he started to scent, pushing his snout under the mattress and trying to dig on top of it in an almost frenzied-like attempt to dig the child out. This was accompanied by his aggressive barking which was his way of telling me that he had found something, which amounted to a harrowing sight. As this was going on, I approached Echo and although he was right in indicating the presence of the child, I wanted him to move on and search for other potential survivors. I took hold of his search harness and pulled him to another part of the collapsed structure and reset him for another search. Although he searched with ease, he was constantly distracted by the child and wanted to return to his location. I felt desperately sorry for this young child and knew Echo was trying his best to make everything right, but that was never going to happen. After 20 minutes or so, I was confident Echo had done his best and as he gave no further indications on potential survivors, I called off his search and handed over to the dog handler from Yorkshire. I wanted to give Ace a go but due to the serious nature of this job it required skilled dogs who knew what they were doing. After briefing the Yorkshire dog team, I went back to my van to clean Echo off. He had sustained a bad cut to his upper front leg that would require a few stitches but otherwise he was ok. I wanted to take a few minutes to reflect on what had just happened and try to clear my thoughts and get back into the present. I kept telling myself that no matter how bad I was feeling, other people around here were feeling a lot worse. As I sat in my van listening to Echo panting vigorously in the back, I wondered how long he could keep up this type of work. He was getting old and Ace was still six months away from attempting his search test. I also thought of my own sanity and all that I had seen over the years. I was not well mentally and had terrible nightmares which were incredibly vivid in content. It seemed a lifetime ago since Echo had been fighting me for the dog toy on our first training event with the police guy, and I knew Echo's days were numbered and Ace needed to step up to the plate and take Echo's place as number 1 USAR dog.

CHAPTER 8

CHANGING TIMES

It was a warm March day in 2013 when Ace passed his assessment as a USAR dog and could finally put on his yellow qualification tag. His assessment was much easier than the one Echo had done years before. Internal politics had watered the process down to a shadow of its former glory, but, that said, he had worked hard for his qualification and, on reflection, had been much easier to train than Echo. He was a pure search machine who was only happy when he was out playing the search game. He was a tough mutt and had no trouble keeping up with me on regular 10-mile mountain bike rides. He was what a search dog should look like, fit, lean and tough. I was proud of Ace and Echo and just a little bit proud of myself for turning out such great search dogs having never ever owned a dog in my life.

Ace quickly became number one search dog, which gave Echo a more backseat position, although Echo was still available for call-out if needed. My time was spent concentrating on Ace, but I did keep Echo's skills up with an occasional search.

By July of 2013, Clare, my dog training assistant, had started to train her own search dog called Buster. In keeping with Manchester fire dog tradition, he was a yellow Labrador and was the son of Ace. A few months earlier, Ace had been involved in an unfortunate incident that resulted in 10 baby Labrador pups, Buster being one of them. Buster was just like his dad, tough and full of life. He joined our dog training sessions with Clare, who was delighted to be a handler with her own dog in training. It was a good period in my life, training had become much more fun than in earlier days and we enjoyed each other's company. Buster would eventually become a fantastic search dog and every bit as good as his dad, a real asset to the Fire

Service and the people of Manchester, but unfortunately politics and management short-sightedness would play a part in his future and his ultimate withdrawal from service. Ace had qualified four months before and had even seen a deployment to a guy who had gone missing in the woods. Echo still tried his best, but his health was fading, and he took an even greater back seat to the now mighty Ace.

July 2013 had been a warm, slow month so far with not much going on for the dog team. Even Lucy was not up to much, which was unusual. I was at home one day just messing about and watching TV, when I got a call from fire control saying that a request from an incident in Rochdale had been received for a search and rescue dog. I asked for the details and I was told that a large, detached house had suddenly exploded, and it was reported that people were missing. The Fire Service were there but search and rescue teams were required which meant Ace and Echo would be needed. I knew that this would be a serious job if search and rescue teams were required. My experience told me that the panic button had been pressed and I knew Lancashire Fire Service search and rescue teams would not be far behind. I ran into the garden and took Ace and Echo out of the kennel they were resting in. I looked at Lucy and wondered, given the cause of this collapse, an explosion, would she be required? Given my experience in fire investigation work with Lucy, I knew buildings general exploded for one of two reasons: a gas explosion or a petrol overpressure. I only had space for two dogs in my van, so decided to leave her until I knew more information.

It took me about 30 minutes to get to the incident site, which was situated on a large housing estate about two miles from the centre of Rochdale. On arrival I could see a large Victorian period house that had exploded with debris thrown over a large area. Fire crews were trying to extinguish several small fires that had started because of the explosion, and the adjacent houses had been damaged, but not so severely. I parked near to our major incident unit and walked over to book in attendance. I was met by one of our fire scene investigation officers, Mark Taylor, who was at the scene to investigate what had happened. He asked if I had Lucy with me as he suspected foul play and had heard reports from the firefighters that they could smell petrol near the scene. I told him I hadn't because of lack of space in my van, but if necessary, I could go back and get her.

After booking in and surveying the scene at close quarters, I attended a multi-agency briefing that was being led by a dangerous building's inspector from the local council; the Fire Service loves a good multi agency meeting. He informed the senior fire officers that the building was too dangerous to let firefighters inside and, due to the nature of the collapse, it was likely that more of the building would come down at any moment. This posed a dilemma for the bosses: we had to get in, and fast, to look for any survivors, but who was going to give the order to go into a building that was ready to collapse at any moment? I saw an opportunity and immediately spoke up. I said that Ace could be deployed within a short time to conduct an initial sweep of the building and give us a good appreciation of what was going on. No firefighters would be put at risk; Ace would work faster and safer than any human could walking on the same structure. He was agile and could get out of trouble as fast as he got into it and it made sense to keep the human firefighters safe and put Ace on the job. This was the perfect solution and, not surprisingly, they went for it. It was a great opportunity for Ace to show his colours.

As I was walking back to my van, search and rescue teams were arriving from Lancashire Fire Service in big lumbering heavy goods vehicles, which only served to block the surrounding streets. Unfortunately, I would not be getting any support from Kurt and Isle from Lancashire dog team on this occasion. They were away and not available for call-out. It was all down to Ace on this one.

I opened the rear doors of my van and decided to take Ace for the now familiar walk to allow him to have a pee and do what he had to before the search got going. Dogs love routine and this formed part of Ace's pre-search one. Echo just sat there hoping he would be required and not left out, I thought of using him, but due to the nature of the collapse it would require agility and fitness from the dog, something that Echo no longer had. It would also be necessary for Ace to wear his search boots on this job as there were large amounts of broken glass and debris that could cause him harm if he stood on them. I also decided to fit his Go Pro harness and camera to record the search from a dog's point of view and to add to the evidence-collection process later down the line. Ace was a great search dog but had no sense whatsoever; his brain had been taken out at birth and replaced with a house brick. He was bone from the neck up, but my God, he could search when he had to!

As I approached the incident with Ace, I was met by a guy called John from Lancashire Fire Service USAR team who was in the early stages of training his own search dog, a big black Labrador called Sid. He wished us both luck and gave Ace a reassuring pat on the head. John eventually became a great search dog handler and a good friend.

Due to the nature and uncertainty of the building, or what was left of it, I decided to work Ace from around the side searching of what remained of the ground floor and then making our way up to what remained of the stairs, which were now totally unsupported and exposed to the outside world as the wall next to them had collapsed. I did a wind direction check with my bottle of talcum powder before I set Ace off; it's important for a search dog to search into the wind if possible, the wind direction was favourable and blowing right into Ace's nose. I also decided to move all the firefighters who had gathered to watch, as I did not want any additional distractions for Ace as he carried out his search.

As I bent over to release his lead, I felt him brace and take the slack out of it. He became hyper vigilant and I could see him scanning the rubble pile with his head darting left and right like some modern-day heat-seeking radar scanning for its next victim. I put my thumb on the release clip and shouted my challenge, "Fire Service search dogs, if you can hear me make a noise". This immediately started Ace barking and desperate to get going. I released the clip, and he went like a greyhound into the search. The rubble had fallen at an awkward angle and Ace found it hard to navigate a safe route up. He eventually decided on a route and went for it. He was moving at a good pace with his nose scanning the rubble, occasionally he would stop and put his nose high in the air to sample what he thought may be a target. When he was happy it was nothing he would continue. I watched him constantly for changes in body language that would let me know he was on to something. After working with a dog for a while you get to read his behaviour, the little things that only you can see in him. After about 10 minutes, I was happy the lower portion of the building had been searched and decided to put Ace into the real danger zone. The stairs were not a safe place to play, but Ace had to go up them. I decided that if Ace was going to take the risk then so was I, as in Haiti years before when Echo panicked on the ladder. I felt we were a team, and we should share the risk and responsibility equally to go up I called him and pointed to the stairs and told him "**up**". He went without hesitation and I followed him dutifully. As I climbed the stairs, I could feel them swaying underneath me. This is not a good idea; I remember thinking to myself. We were both up the stairs in less than 10 seconds, but it felt a lifetime when they could have collapsed at any moment.

Once at the top, I told Ace to search all available areas which he was already doing darting in and out of partly-collapsed rooms and even managing to fall through the floor at one point, but luckily only falling a few feet before shaking himself off and getting on with the job. As Ace was searching, I could definitely detect a mild petrol odour and wondered where it was coming from. After Ace had searched all the available areas that he could, I called the search off because it's always possible that if you keep your dog going over the same areas time and time again, he will eventually start to think that someone is there and start barking. This is called a false indication and is basically caused by poor dog handling skills. Given the fact Ace had not located anyone, I decided that was enough.

After I had departed the collapsed building via the dodgy staircase and a good check of Ace after his fall through the floor, I found the Fire Investigation guy, Mark, who was still in the command vehicle. I told him that he was right, and I could smell some form of accelerant while in the building. I also told him that now I had seen the devastated building from a new perspective when I'd searched the top floor, the explosion looked very much like a petrol overpressure and not a gas explosion. A petrol overpressure is a result of petrol vapour exploding with such force that it can destroy even the strongest structures surrounding it, and it doesn't take that much petrol to achieve this.

Following a brief discussion with Mark about the best way to find out if the explosion was a result of gas or an overpressure from poured petrol, he asked me to go and collect Lucy. As I drove down the M60 towards my home, I had time to reflect on the job I had just done, and the risks taken in following Ace up the stairs and into the danger zone. I found myself in an uncomfortable place and had to pull off at the first services area I came across to get my head together. I had taken some unbelievable risks during the earthquakes in Haiti and other areas around the world in support of Echo's search work but had got away with it time and time again, it was now dawning on me that these risks I seem to be still taking were at some point going to bite me on the bum, and my luck was going to run out.

After composing myself, I arrived home and loaded Lucy into my van. I left Echo and took Ace back to the job, as he may have been required again at some point.

I returned to the incident and it was obvious that due to Ace's efforts things had started to calm down a bit, as he had not indicated the presence of anyone trapped. I again met up with Mark and he asked me the question I did not want to be asked but knew was coming. He asked if I would be prepared to go back into the building with Lucy, this time to hunt for this elusive smell of petrol. Initially, I said no as I was willing to risk myself and Ace to save a life, but to take the risk to find petrol was too much to ask. After some discussions, I decided that if this issue was going to be resolved in the near future then I would need to get Lucy to work, so I reluctantly agreed to go back in.

I set Lucy off in the same position as I had with Ace. This time it would not be as risky, as search and rescue firefighters had shored up the staircase by means of large wooden props so the chance of it collapsing under me was very much reduced. As Lucy ran up the stairs, I knew she was on to a scent; I could read this dog like a book. She ran to the top and then veered off to the right just as Ace had done. I hoped she would not fall down the same hole as Ace had, to be honest, she did have more sense than Ace. As I reached the top of the stairs, I could see Lucy was very busy in an area which, prior to the explosion, had been a bedroom. I thought that we are on to something here and, as she worked her way into the remains of the room, her nose was glued to the floor with the thudding sound that I called the freight train nose. After no more than a few seconds, she found what she was hunting for, her body braced like a stiff statue-like figure, her nose was pointing, and she was totally focused on the carpet; her eyes transfixed to a spot no bigger than a one pence piece. Lucy was a very athletic dog and had a muscular physique way beyond that of a normal pet Labrador. When she indicated in this passive silent manner, she looked impressive, almost chiselled out of stone. I moved closer to her and noted the very spot she had indicated; I then gave one click on the clicker I carried, which in turn let Lucy know that she had found what she was looking for and it was now time to play. She had been trained to find around 20 different types of liquid accelerants, so I knew her indication meant something important.

As I left the building, I spoke with Mark and told him what Lucy had found and that it was over to him now to finish the job. He was relieved and thanked us for our efforts. He asked if we could hang about for a while, in case she was needed again, but by this time I was totally exhausted and I felt that Ace and Lucy had done what was required of them and it was time to leave for home.

That evening, while drinking a nice glass of red wine, I smiled to myself about the great work the dogs had done that day. Ace had conducted a search in a building too dangerous for human firefighters to enter and his efforts had kept them out of harm's way and safe. Lucy had basically cracked the case and made the fire investigation team's work much easier in determining the cause of the explosion, and the public had been reassured that the Fire Service was pulling out all the stops by bringing in the dog team. It was great work by the dogs and one in the eye for those in the Fire Service who thought the dogs were a waste of time.

A few days later, I found out the cause of this incident: basically, the house had been a hostel type of accommodation, a disgruntled resident had tried to commit suicide by pouring petrol all over the place but had not banked on the amount of vapour released by this action. When a lighter was lit the petrol didn't burn, but rather exploded in a violent and destructive manner causing the building to collapse. It looked like my observations from the upstairs of the property had been correct and a petrol overpressure was the cause. And in case you are wondering, the guy who committed the crime in an attempt to kill himself survived!

The months and years that followed these events were marred by industrial unrest in the Fire Service nationally. Ace and Buster had been prevented from taking over from Echo on the international search and rescue team for one trivial reason or another and were destined to be a UK asset only. This upset me as I knew Ace was a top search dog, but I was resigned to the fact that this was the deal. My enthusiasm was also dwindling for this type of overseas work. In my 25 years on the overseas response team, I had learned that it consisted of two types of people: those that genuinely wanted to help and be part of something for the good of others, and those who were just interested in being in the limelight and using it as a platform for showing off how good they thought they were. I had done with it.

Around 2015, it was announced by the National Resilience Committee, (this was the organisation that oversaw search and rescue operations for the UK government), that Manchester Fire Services funding for search and rescue would be withdrawn, and they could rely on surrounding fire services to provide a search capability if it was required. This meant that our dog team, funded via central government, would also disappear. It was a strange proposal given that Manchester was a major city in the UK, both strategically and economically, with a history of terrorist activities going back as far as the 1970s. But to my disgust and to the detriment of the fantastic people of Manchester, who, my dog team was tasked to protect, the government funding for the search and rescue dog capability was withdrawn, with, in my opinion, little opposition from the Fire Service locally.

Ace was now stateless, so to speak. I decided that as Manchester needed a search and rescue dog, no matter what other people may say, I would keep Ace available to the service for free, at no cost to the Fire Service and the taxpayer. My brother who was an ex-fire officer said I was stupid and that I should just retire Ace and leave it at that if that's what they wanted. I dug my heels in and said no, the public of Manchester deserve better. Buster had already been side-lined due to politics and I was determined that if Manchester got hit again with a terror attack, Ace would play his part in rescuing people.

This is where writing this book gets difficult. A Fire Service have a duty to be ready for all eventualities, and I mean "all" eventualities. At the beginning of 2016, I was told in no uncertain terms that Ace was no longer to be made available for call out. He was to retire with immediate effect and consigned to the history books. I pleaded with the managers in the service that this was a big mistake, and his skills would be required in the future. I knew having seen buildings collapse abroad, and the totally destructive nature of such events, that only dogs could be effective in locating trapped people, but these desperate words fell on deaf ears. Please excuse me if you think I'm being too passionate or protective of the dog capability I had created, but the years of earthquakes and the PTSD had taught me one important thing: if the worst can happen, it probably will.

At 10.31pm on the 22nd of May 2017, a suicide bomber detonated an improvised explosive device at a concert at the Manchester Arena. This resulted in the deaths of 22 people and over 800 being hospitalised. My son, Daniel, phoned me and told me to turn on to Sky News as something had happened at the arena. As I looked at the TV and read the updates flashing across the bottom of the screen, my anger finally boiled over. I screamed and punched the wall in our front room. This situation was exactly what Echo and Ace had been trained for, this is what the years of search experience and constant training was designed to prepare us for. It was to protect people and to ensure that in the event of exactly this type of incident, the Fire Service could respond with appropriate assets and equipment, dogs being part of that response. I cursed the decision to withdraw Ace from service and shouted in anger at the TV. Sue came rushing down from upstairs to ask what was going on and why all the shouting. I hugged her hard and just kept saying over and over that it had finally happened. We both sat looking in disbelief at the updates, I felt empty and cold. I had designed this dog team to be ready for anything, to respond at a moment's notice to support and most importantly to protect the people of Manchester in the direst of situations. This was the most tragic situation I could imagine; I was sick to my stomach knowing that my search dog team had been consigned to the history books only months before.

CHAPTER 9

IN THE PICTURE

In June 2018, I was informed that my two service dogs, Lucy and Echo, were to receive the PDSA Order of Merit, the animal equivalent of the OBE. This was a total surprise and a great honour. To have one dog on our team win was fantastic, to have two was outstanding.

Echo had been nominated for his actions on overseas deployments and operational work within Greater Manchester as well as his outstanding dedication to the people of Greater Manchester.

Lucy had been nominated for her contribution to over 200 years of prison time for arson-related crime and her outstanding contribution to community fire safety initiatives in the Manchester area.

By this time, Lucy had retired to her new home in France and Echo was a very old boy whose glory days were long past. I was informed that a representative from the PDSA awards team was going to make contact with me with details of what would happen next.

I had a vision of what this contact would look like, maybe a Barbara Woodhouse type of lady who would bark orders at me and the dogs expecting instant compliance, or a Victoria Stilwell type dressed in tight black leather. Secretly, I was hoping for the tight black leather one!

On the day of our first meeting, I arranged to meet Amy from the PDSA at our headquarters in Manchester. We agreed to meet early, so we would have the chance to talk about the dogs and how we were going to move this award forward. As I was waiting in reception for her, I had a nervous feeling in my stomach, almost like the butterflies one gets before a first date. I had not seen Amy yet and still feared the worst. As I sat on the comfy chairs that surrounded the entrance to our HQ, I noticed a car pull up at the barrier outside. As the buzzer on the intercom sounded, I knew that this was it; the moment of truth had arrived. This was her and I felt for some reason completely at her mercy.

After Amy had parked up, I went out to meet her and to my surprise and relief she was not at all what I expected. She was about 5ft 6ins tall and very slim with soft features, very pretty with a 'girl next door' look about her. I was disappointed about the lack of tight leather, but you win some, you lose some.

When all the introductions had been done, I escorted Amy into the HQ building and up to my office. I informed all my workmates who she was and why she was here. The first thing she wanted to know was all about the dogs, personalities, and information about the work they did, a real in-depth look into the workings of a modern search and rescue dog in the Fire Service. I found this very comforting, talking about my dogs in a positive way to someone who really wanted to know the real me and the real dogs. I gave Amy a 'warts and all' account of what it took to be a Fire Service dog. This was important as I felt this award was not just about my dog-team but was representative of all the dogs and handlers that I had trained with, dedicated professionals prepared to put themselves on the line if necessary. After a couple of hours hearing me talk about the dogs, I suggested we went down to the canteen that we had at our HQ for some lunch. It was staffed by some great individuals who turned out fantastic food, it was also cheap so a win/win for me.

As we chatted, I felt more at ease with Amy. My fears had turned to real joy at having her deal with my dogs and the upcoming awards. She explained that a day would be organised to get some photographs of the dogs and make a short film about Echo and Lucy to show on the night of the awards ceremony. It all sounded very exciting and only what these hero dogs deserved.

After lunch was done and all the chat complete, Amy gave me some dates for the pictures and filming to take place and said she would keep in touch with any developments. As we bade our goodbyes, I felt another corner had been turned in the story of Echo, but this time he had dragged his sidekick Lucy along with him.

As I lay in bed that evening, I thought of how fantastic this all was, my dog team had now bagged the Pride of Britain as part of the Manchester team, the IFAW Animal of the Year, and now the highly prestigious PDSA Order of Merit. I slept well that night.

About two weeks later, the day arrived for the PDSA to come over to Manchester and indulge in some interviews and photographs of Echo. Lucy was, by this time, living in France so took no part in the proceedings. However, by sheer luck, I did have some great pictures of her and some moving film that I had taken while she was on a job which I gave to Amy and the film crew accompanying her.

I met them all at the service training centre, as I wanted a real 'Fire Service feel' to the event. Amy gave a short brief as to how the day was going to run starting with some photographs being taken of Echo with his medal and a short interview with me outlining what Echo and Lucy were like and how we had bonded to make such a great search team. A short movie would then be filmed showing Echo running about, this bit made me smile to myself as Echo was nearly 15 and his days of running about were long gone. In all this excitement and anticipation, the one thing that I had not seen yet was the medal itself. The honour of winning an award like the Order of Merit is a once-in-a-lifetime achievement, or you could say twice in our case as we had two dogs receiving it, but the real thrill for me was the actual medal itself; something my dogs could actually wear round their necks to show how heroic and meaningful their lives had been. As I could see Amy was busy organising things, I asked her assistant what the medals looked like, she looked at me with a vague look on her face and said that the medals were actually there, and that Amy had them in her bag. I immediately asked if I could see them as the suspense was killing me. We walked over to where Amy was just having a brew, and the assistant asked her if I could see the medals. She agreed at once and apologised for not showing me earlier. She said she only had Echo's and as Lucy was not with me, she hadn't brought it along. As she reached into her bag a feeling of almost unbelievable joy came over me. This is what it was all about, more recognition, not just for my dogs but Fire Service dogs everywhere. Amy then handed me a small blue box. My hands trembled as I opened it to reveal a fantastically shiny silver medal with a long blue and white medal ribbon attached to it. It had Echo's name on the front and written on the back was "for operations in Haiti 2010". All the years of toil and suffering had suddenly come to a head; it was as if the open door that had been Echo and Lucy's lives had suddenly been closed in this final act of recognition. I tried to hold the tears back, but it was no good. I had to let my emotions run free.

The day went very well with all the necessary pictures and interviews completed to everyone's satisfaction; Echo even managed a short run for the film crew.

The day of the awards ceremony was approaching fast. We had been informed that Lucy was going to come over from France for the event with her adopted parents, which was great news, I thought. Echo had not seen Lucy for at least 18 months since she left for retirement on the continent. We were also informed that a dog from British Transport police called Mojo, who was used in the aftermath of the arena bombing, was also going to be honoured.

The day of the awards arrived, it was to take place at the Old Trafford Cricket ground conference suite and was due to start at around 7.30pm. I gave Echo a bath and combed his hair to make him look the hero he had come to be. I was also looking forward to meeting Lucy again and wondered if the dogs would recognise each other. My son Daniel and his partner Jenny were also attending, so it was a real family affair. I had not had much luck in securing a senior officer from the Fire Service to accompany me to this prestigious event, my requests having fallen on deaf ears. I was even more shocked when I saw the top boss from the transport police arrive with Mojo and his handler. Luckily, at the 11th hour, a pal of mine who was in charge of the ISAR team in Manchester offered to come along and support me. It would have been very embarrassing stood on the stage on my own.

I got to the cricket ground early so I could work out what the score was. One side issue with my PTSD was that I got very anxious very quickly, so having a walk through the night's events was a good start to the evening. Sue was looking fantastic in the new dress she bought for the occasion and I was looking a bit dapper in my best Fire Service dress uniform. My first port of call was Amy from the PDSA, who was looking fantastic as usual and calmed me down with some reassuring words. I was surprised at how many people were there, many more than I expected. It was also good to see life size images of Echo and Lucy, as well as Mojo on the walls and surrounding the stage. It made you feel like you were in the presence of some true K9 heroes. After a short time, I was informed by Daniel that Lucy had arrived and was on her way up. I was so excited to be with her again. We had been a team for nearly 10 years fighting arson-related crime all over the north west of England.

I saw Paul, Lucy's new dad. I shook his hand and asked where the old girl was. He said she couldn't climb the stairs, so his partner Debbie was bringing her up in the lift. How the mighty fall, I thought. When Lucy finally entered the room, it was like a light had been turned on in Echo's head. He pulled at his lead to get over to her, they nosed each other for about 20 seconds then Echo started licking her face. It was such a terrific and emotional moment, just too difficult to describe. Everyone was stood in admiration for the love these dogs still had for each other.

When all the introductions had been completed, it was time for the proceedings to get underway, the lights dimmed and as it was Echo's turn to go first, a chilling video came on the screen outlining his career. As I watched it, Sue squeezed my hand and gave me a reassuring smile. I was incredibly proud and felt people in the room staring at me as Echo did his bit on the screen. Did we really do this? I thought. The real Echo had actually fallen asleep at my feet. After the film, the chairperson from the PDSA gave a short speech about Echo and the medal and how it had been won. It was then time for Echo and me to go on stage to get the award. When they called us forward, I first had to wake Echo up which I did with a slight tug on his lead. He didn't seem too keen to get up, but he slowly got to his feet and accompanied me to the stage. He couldn't climb the stage staircase, so I lifted him on which filled my nice black uniform full of dog hairs. The medal was placed around his neck like he was some form of Olympic champion. I asked if I could say a few words which it turned out was a mistake, as the emotion of the moment hit me, and the words just would not come out. Fortunately, my service chaperon for the evening jumped in and spoke on my behalf which saved the day.

Next up was Lucy. Again, a short film was followed by a few words about her career and life working with the fire investigation team and for the second time emotion tugged at my heart strings. Giving Lucy up on her retirement was a hard decision, but it was the right one to make. Paul and his partner had given her everything she wanted and loved her as much as anyone could have. When Lucy was called forward, Paul came with her to give her some reassurance. The medal was placed round her neck and that concluded the official part of the evening. It was time to mingle and meet some of the big wigs from the PDSA charity.

As we chatted about the dogs' antics overseas and in the UK, it became apparent how much they meant to people, the work they do and the hearts they touch along the way. Echo and Lucy sat next to each other the whole-time, tails wagging. I went over to Mojo's handler and congratulated him on his award and thanked him for his efforts on that tragic night at the arena. He was a nice guy.

After about an hour, I could see Echo and Lucy had fallen asleep next to each other, just as they had when they lived in my back yard. I asked Sue if she was ready to go and she said that it had been a long day and home was calling. We arranged to meet Paul and Debbie outside together with Lucy. I wanted the goodbyes to be private, so I thanked all at the PDSA for a great evening. It had been a great success.

When we got outside it was just starting to go dark. Lucy was already in the back of Paul's car with the rear door still up. I lifted Echo up so they could have a last sniff, because I knew that they would never see each other again. We had been a team for 10 years, the three musketeers saving life and fighting crime. I knew this was it. I held Lucy one last time and told her to be a good girl. As I drove away, I could see her looking at us through the back window. When I got home, I poured a glass of wine and listened to the *Never-Ending Story* by Limahl, but I knew that all stories come to an end at some point, As will this story.

EPILOGUE

Well, all that was a while ago now. I'm now retired from the fire brigade after 30 year's service, 17 of them working with my fantastic dog team. I have to say that I am very lucky to have served in such an incredible role within the Fire Service. I served in the USAR team under the banner of New Dimensions, I was on the ISAR team which took me all over the world on fantastic adventures, and I designed, and implemented, a K9 capability for our fire investigation team. I didn't really mention Lucy, my fire dog, that much in this book, but believe me, that's another story to be told.

I was diagnosed with PTSD in 2012 and the years that followed were tough on my wife, as my condition deteriorated considerably. I kept my issues from my work colleagues, but I was slowly bleeding to death mentally, in the end, having had thoughts about ending my life to ease the pain, I sought help. The Fire Service are years behind when it comes to PTSD issues and I got the feeling they wanted me and the condition as far away from them as possible. Whenever I tried to explain the type of situations you can find yourself in, especially overseas on operations, my descriptions were just dismissed as fantasy and delusion, the rantings of a man too caught up in a situation too difficult to understand by those who have never experienced it. I was told by one individual that if I brought the extent of my condition to the attention of the service, I could have my card marked, so 'keep it to yourself'. Not a helpful comment, but I took the hint. It took a long time to clear my head and reassure myself that I had done all I could in mostly hopeless situations. It was mainly due to the patience and support of my wife and a guy called Chris, who walked me through the recovery phase and, to be honest, saved my life. I will always be grateful Chris for your support and compassion.

So, what happened to the main people in the book? Clare, my dog training buddy, and handler of Buster is now in the last few years of her Fire Service career. She still works at our Technical Response station. Buster qualified as a search and rescue dog and was fantastic at it, a real hunter, but before he could take his place next to Ace, cutbacks and short sightedness by managers in the Fire Service, cut his career off before it started, but he's still a much loved part of Clare's family and a great pet dog.

Daniel, my son, and right-hand man for dog training is now a duty manager of a gym in the Manchester area and lives with his partner who is a solicitor. He's now tall and slender with dark features, a far cry from the young boy who I saw playing with Echo at my dad's years before. He always said that the years he spent dog training were the best of his life so far and he never regrets getting involved. Could not have done it without you, Daniel.

Sue, my long-suffering wife, still works for the Fire Service but longs for retirement and the peace that it brings. She's had enough turmoil in her life. She splits her time with me either in our lodge in Somerset or our camper van travelling in Europe when we get the opportunity. She's proud of what I did, but when asked says, defiantly "no more dogs in the Dewar house".

Now let's take a look at the main players in the story, the dogs themselves.

Lucy, the fire dog, worked until she was 12 and was very much the unsung hero of our dog team. I may write a book about her exploits one day, every bit as tragic and dramatic as Echo's tale. On retirement, she was taken on by a retired firefighter and his partner who live in Northern France on a smallholding. Lucy passed away peacefully in October 2020 with her adopted parents by her side. It was a great comfort to me that she was not alone when she died.

What became of Ace the crazy Lab that I acquired as an unwanted pet. He's now retired, and his blond locks of hair are now grey. His chiseled physique has dropped, and he mopes about most days with an empty plastic bottle in his mouth. It was a crying shame that he was massively underused by the Fire Service, both locally and nationally, but that was the politics of the day. He still lives with me and Sue, but again the years of heavy work have taken a toll on him. He hobbles around now but is still active and responsive when he sees a tennis ball.

And then the mighty Echo, the hero of this story, the best dog any person could have asked for, the dog, if you remember, I wanted to get rid of. It was only Sue's insistence on keeping him that he became the hero he did. Well, Echo's not with us anymore I'm sorry to say. He retired in 2013 and took a back seat to Ace. As the years marched on, Echo became a much-loved family pet and regularly accompanied me on my public speaking engagements when I regaled stories of his heroics overseas. He became a firm favorite of many a ladies' group and college student. He also enjoyed time at the caravan we owned in Wales and, although unable to walk with ease, always managed to make it down to the beach for a play, even though I had to carry him back.

As the weeks turned to months and the months to years Echo's health started to suffer. The arteritis in his legs made even getting up a struggle, but if he was comfortable, he was happy. We moved him into the front room and out of his garden kennel to give him a rest from the other dogs and keep him warm in the winter months, he sat on his mat in front of the TV and became an immovable obstacle.

They say that when your dog is ready to go, they will let you know. I always wanted Echo to pass away in the night warm on his bed, and when I got up, he would be gone. Is that not what we all want? But I knew it was never going to be that easy.

Around the beginning of June 2019, I noticed that he was wetting himself and even soiling himself at times. Sue was busy cleaning him one day when I suggested we have a talk about his future, Sue said she would not discuss anything like that because she knew what I was suggesting, and that Echo would be ok. I just left it at that but knew this was hurting Sue a lot.

Near the end of June 2019, we took Echo to our caravan. We knew that if the weather was good, he could spend the days outside lying on the grass and chilling out. At this point he could not even get back into the caravan without assistance and to be honest was getting worse by the day. The weather was good, and Echo just sat on his mat in the sun, only raising his head to see what was going around him. Ace occasionally came over to him to lick his ears or lay next to him for a while. It was obvious that both me and Sue were in total denial about Echo's condition and didn't even discuss it anymore. The thought of him not being here devastated me; he was my last link to the horrors of Haiti, and I was fearful of the consequences of him passing, on my own mental health.

I woke early on the 5th of July. It was sunny outside; my mind was surprisingly clear. I had not slept much the night before, so went straight outside with a coffee to soak up some sun. After coming in from the garden, I noticed that Echo had soiled himself badly during the night and was just lay in it all. I also noticed for the first time how thin he had become. I had been determined not to notice this in the previous weeks, so had put it out of my mind. Now it was time to face facts. As I entered the room, I lay down next to him and just stroked his head, he looked at me and at that point I knew what he was telling me. 'It's time dad, you need to let me go'. I phoned Sue and told her to come home from work as I needed support, and we needed to speak. When she arrived, I told her that Echo had finally let me know that it was time he left us. She just stared at me and said nothing. I had already spoken to the vets and made all the arrangements. It was booked for 7th July at 11am. I told Sue not to argue with me this time. I knew we had already left it far too long to come to this decision.

We spent our last night with Echo just lying on the floor stroking him and talking to him, telling him how much we loved him and how he had totally changed our lives. To be honest, it was surreal. Daniel and his girlfriend came down to say their goodbyes, Daniel was shaking as he held Echo, the way he held him years before as a pup. He said 'goodbye, brother' and placed his head back gently on the pillow. I found that I was now totally ready for Echo's passing and, as I sat on the floor looking into his eyes, I could see images of Haiti looking back at me. This scared me but I knew this was Echo's last act of kindness towards me. I like to think he was trying to purge his own memories of this tragic event and put my own terrible nightmares to bed forever.

The next morning, the 7th of July 2019, Sue and I tried to busy ourselves. Echo was due at the vets at 11am so we stayed at home till about 10am. Sue eventually said it was time to go and I knew this was it. I wrapped Echo up in a large Fire Service flag and carried him into our front garden for a wee. He hobbled about for a while and eventually had his wee. I said to Sue that this was the last time he was going to be in his home, the last time we were going to be together as a family. She told me to stop making it hard on myself and just get on with it. I carried him to the van and placed the flag back over him to keep him warm, and we set off. We didn't speak at all on the journey and just sat with our own thoughts and memories.

When we arrived at the vets, they took us into a private room and told us we had as long as we wanted with Echo and to let them know when we were ready. I didn't know what to say, words failed me at this important moment, I looked at him with an overwhelming feeling of total love. I will always love you Echo, you were my friend and workmate, you changed my life, you never let me down and I hope I did the same for you, I will miss you every day until the time comes when we can run again together, I knew that I was going to have total breakdown very soon and I could see that Sue, although trying to hold it together, was going down fast.

After about 10 minutes, I went out and told them we were ready. They came for Echo and told us to wait in the family room for a minute or two and they would then call us into the consultation room. After a while the vet came in and asked us to follow her into the next room. When we went in, I could see Echo lying on a high metal table with a blanket over half his body and a tube in his leg. He was sat up and just looking about, I went over to him and he licked my hand which was more than I could take. I just broke down in total floods of tears, as did Sue. I told him that this was it, a great adventure is waiting for you my boy, a new adventure to add to your long list and it would not be long until I joined him, and we could be together again. The vet asked if we were ready. I looked at Sue and she just nodded at me, so I said, "Yes, let's do it." Sue held him and I held his head and looked directly into his eyes as the vet pushed on the syringe to administer the lethal dose. Be brave Echo, as brave as you have been in life. His head went heavy and he lay on his side, his eyes closed for the last time and, in that moment, a part of me died as well.

So, what does the future hold now it's all over? I have found employment as a cruise line enrichment speaker working for a major cruise line. Telling stories about myself and Echo's adventures around the world, I get good crowds, and to be honest, I enjoy telling people about this fantastic dog and how he helped so many people and touched so many hearts. I also have a painting of Echo that sits with pride on my wall at home, it depicts him in an earthquake zone and in his full glory. It's daft I know, but I find myself talking to it sometimes.

On occasions when cruising, after the events of the evening are over, I find a quiet corner of the ship, usually on the top deck looking out to sea. I sit with a large glass of red wine and just listen to the wind making its way slowly past the boat and then disappearing into the night. My mind drifts to distant places and adventures now long gone and the new ones to come. I was once asked in an interview if being a dog handler in the Fire Service was worth all the problems that it caused me over the years; the PTSD, the long hours away from home and family and the restrictions it placed on my promotion and career prospects. I gave the following answer.

For some yes, it is worth it, for others I don't know, you will have to ask them that question, but for me personally... No regrets!

I was Echo. A New Dimension.